MW00593812

"Silence is necessary for a true sac[...] personal encounter with the Livin[...] are at a loss for words. Who woul[...] Almighty? For this reason, I am p[...]r[...] the reading of this *St. Faustina Prayer Book for Adoration*. May St. Faustina's wisdom help us tame the 'dictatorship of noise' through silencing our eyes and ears in order that for our hearts 'faith provides a supplement for the failure of the senses'!"

— CARDINAL ROBERT SARAH
Prefect of the Congregation for Divine Worship
and the Discipline of the Sacraments, Rome

"This stunning and powerful book can help you better appreciate and follow the stepping stones to a deeper adoration St. Faustina discovered and developed in her own life. Here are ways to lift you to a new supernatural level, to a more personal and intimate relationship with Our Lord."

— JACQUELYN LINDSEY
Editor of *LEAVES* magazine

"The future of humanity will be greatly influenced by those who take time for adoration of the Blessed Sacrament. Susan Tassone's *St. Faustina Prayer Book for Adoration* provides a spiritual master's guide as to why adoration will make a difference in one's spiritual life and the world. This book will awaken a deeper desire for disciples of Christ to find their way to a church or chapel in the spirit of St. Faustina and allow her to become a great mentor in the art of adoration. Thank you, Susan Tassone, for honing the depths of St. Faustina's writings to help others discover in a fuller way the Lord of the Eucharist, who awaits our time alone with Him!"

— MOST REVEREND ROBERT J. BAKER
Bishop of Birmingham

"Perhaps no other devotional practice offers greater opportunity for transformation than Eucharistic Adoration. In her latest book, best-selling author Susan Tassone offers us the wisdom, insight, and inspiration of St. Faustina Kowalska as a means to help us mine the treasury of grace that awaits us before the Sacred Species. Replete with beautiful quotations, practical advice and counsel, and the saint's own prayers and meditations, this prayer book may well become a standard for Eucharistic adorers everywhere."

— JOHNNETTE S. BENKOVIC
EWTN Television and Radio Host
Founder and President of *Women of Grace*®

"With *St. Faustina Prayer Book for Adoration*, author Susan Tassone has given the Church a splendid work to help all of us in the pursuit of holiness. Whether you're just beginning adoration as a discipline or have practiced it for years, through her spirit-filled reflections Susan offers St. Faustina as a companion to accompany and guide you."

— MOST REVEREND JEROME E. LISTECKI
Archbishop of Milwaukee

"*St. Faustina Prayer Book for Adoration* is a rich spiritual guide for those who value quiet time before the Lord in the Blessed Sacrament. This compendium by Susan Tassone will be of great value especially to the iGen culture since many of those born after 1995 are only now discovering how Eucharistic Adoration sets them on a new path for their life. Many seminarians today tell me that their vocational call was first heard during their time spent before the Lord in adoration."

— FATHER MARK A. LATCOVICH, PH.D.
President-Rector of Borromeo and Saint Mary Seminaries
Diocese of Cleveland

"*St. Faustina Prayer Book for Adoration* does a breathtaking job of presenting the words *and* actions of a saint so well-known and admired for her prayer life and devotion to Our Lord. Here's how to focus your own mind and heart on Him as you open your soul to His Divine Mercy."

— Brother Donald Thielsen, O.F.M. Conv.
National Shrine of St. Maximilian Kolbe at Marytown

"I am absolutely convinced that today we must turn to Eucharistic Adoration to be strengthened for the battles of our day. Susan Tassone gives us prayers, insights, gazes, and so much more to help us live Eucharistic-centered lives. Ours is an age of noise. Unless we return to silence in our lives, we will not be able to withstand the chaos of the world. It gave me great joy to find Susan's section on the 'graces of silence' included in this book.

— Most Reverend James D. Conley
Bishop of Lincoln

"*St. Faustina Prayer Book for Adoration* is a precious resource that aids us all as we ponder the mysteries of salvation. Susan Tassone has provided us with an excellent and well-researched guide that enhances our approach to prayer, enriches our awareness of the adoration experience, and transforms our hearts toward holiness."

— Marcel Fredericks, Ph.D.
Professor Emeritus, Loyola University Chicago
Doctor Honoris Causa, Czestochowa University of Technology, Poland

"When, where, and how can you step away from our hectic world's nearly constant noise and enter the peace and silence of adoration? Using selected prayers, insights, and examples from St. Faustina, author Susan Tassone gives you ways to find times, places, and methods to better focus your attention and love on Our Lord. Here, too — living in a merciless world — is how to seek and to share mercy freely as 'The Apostle of Mercy' leads you ever more closely to Jesus."

— FATHER MITCH PACWA, S.J.
Author of *Saved: A Bible Study Guide for Catholics*

"This prayer book is a treasure for anyone who spends time worshiping the Lord in the Blessed Sacrament. Especially unique and valuable are St. Faustina's reflections on adoration and her moving prayers. You'll want to take it with you to the Eucharistic chapel or have it handy at home for spiritual adoration when you can't get there."

— BERT GHEZZI
Author of *The Power of Daily Prayer*

"*St. Faustina Prayer Book for Adoration* is the crown jewel in Susan Tassone's trilogy on St. Faustina and Divine Mercy. Here's why, how, when, and where to offer adoration just as St. Faustina did."

— FATHER DAN CAMBRA, M.I.C.
Holy Souls Sodality at The National Shrine of The Divine Mercy

St. Faustina Prayer Book
for Adoration

Susan Tassone

Our Sunday Visitor

www.osv.com
Our Sunday Visitor Publishing Division
Our Sunday Visitor, Inc.
Huntington, Indiana 46750

Nihil Obstat
Msgr. Michael Heintz, Ph.D.
Censor Librorum

Imprimatur
✠ Kevin C. Rhoades
Bishop of Fort Wayne-South Bend
November 20, 2017

The *Nihil Obstat* and *Imprimatur* are official declarations that a book is free from doctrinal or moral error. It is not implied that those who have granted the *Nihil Obstat* and *Imprimatur* agree with the contents, opinions, or statements expressed.

Our Sunday Visitor Publishing Division, Our Sunday Visitor, Inc.,
200 Noll Plaza, Huntington, IN 46750; 1-800-348-2440

ISBN: 978-1-68192-136-5 (Inventory No. T1861)
eISBN: 978-1-68192-137-2
LCCN: 2017961128

Cover design: Tyler Ottinger
Cover concept: Garrett Fosco
Cover images: Copyright © Marian Fathers of the Immaculate Conception of the B.V.M. Used with permission; Dreamstime and Shutterstock.
Interior design: Sherri L. Hoffman

PRINTED IN THE UNITED STATES OF AMERICA

This book is dedicated to you, My Dear Loyal Readers,
my fellow Prayer Warriors for the Holy Souls.

You've accompanied me, you've walked with me, in freeing souls
from purgatory and giving them the infinite gift of God, the
Beatific Vision. Together, we've helped them reach heaven!

I'm so pleased and humbled to be a part of this wonderful
team. We are the "two or three gathered" in His name,
and Our Lord, Divine Mercy, is with us.

And, as you well know, so is St. Faustina.

With much affection and prayers for you
and for the souls of your dearly departed,

SUSAN

———

Table of Contents

Editor's note: Citations at the end of quotations refer to numbered sections of the *Diary of St. Maria Faustina Kowalska*. For example, see "(441)" on page 22.

Personal Acknowledgments

I'm delighted to share with you some very special heroes in my life. Without them this awesome book wouldn't have been possible!

To Jaymie Stuart Wolfe. My OSV editor and supporter. It was so helpful having a partner as we navigated the book to its finish.

To Jill Adamson. My OSV Senior Trade Marketing Leader. You're beyond amazing, wearing so many hats as you make my works — and "The Purgatory Lady" — known throughout the world. Thank you!

To Bill Dodds. My favorite copy editor. This is our fourth book together and, once again, you went above and beyond what I could imagine. Awe-inspiring! You truly live up to your OSV nickname: "The Master." You helped make this book exquisite ... and a sure best-seller. My deepest thanks!

To Father Dan Cambra, M.I.C. My dear friend and persistent, gracious hero who goes out of his way to make sure everything is on track between Our Sunday Visitor and the Marians. You made the St. Faustina Trilogy possible and will always have a special place in my heart.

To Steven Jay Gross. As St. Paul says, there are no words deep enough to express my gratitude. For close to four decades now, you've always been there for me. Always. You're my champion. Like St. Faustina, you help me get closer to becoming a saint. I couldn't do this without you. Infinite thanks. And special thanks to your wife, Carol Gross, who cheers for me behind the scenes.

To Deacon Mike McCloskey. You're so kind, so helpful. I don't know what I'd do without your outstanding help.

To Sister Claudia Radzewicz, MChR. You were a whiz at locating St.

Faustina's favorite song. Not an easy feat. I'm most grateful for your assistance.

To Father Kazimierz Chwalek, M.I.C. You wouldn't accept an ordinary translation of St. Faustina's song, but retranslated all four verses. The most poetic and touching translation for all the world to read. And you sang it too. Thank you!

To George Foster. Even with one arm in a sling this year, you still spent time after hours and on weekends meticulously going over my manuscript, making sure every *i* was dotted and every *t* was crossed. I appreciate that so much. You're the best!

To Loyola University Chicago Library Head, Dr. Yolande Wersching, and Vanessa Crouther. My extraordinary researchers who always find just what I need to make my work a success. I'm so grateful that I have you both!

To Jean Studer. You always lend me your ear and offer good advice. Thank you.

To Maria Faber. I am grateful for your help in finding the other favorite song of St. Faustina. You always come through and are a special friend.

To Garrett Fosco. Your beautiful cover design captures the essence of this book! Thank you very much.

To the heroes behind the heroes. I've been an author with Our Sunday Visitor for twenty years. While I haven't met all the staff personally, I so appreciate what all of you do for me … and for the holy souls. You've helped make my books award-winning best-sellers.

A Personal Note from the Author

Dear Friends,

You were created by God for adoration. In your heart and in your soul. (As St. Augustine wrote, "You have made us for yourself, O Lord, and our hearts are restless until they find their rest in you.")

You, with your unique, literally one-of-a-kind relationship with God — because He made you unique, literally one of a kind. Body and soul.

And God. Infinite. Eternal All-loving. Calling you, inviting you, to spend time with Him. Just you and Him. Not equals, but Creator and created being He *chose* to create. The one He had in mind, not just since you were conceived but forever.

Quite the pair. God, your Heavenly Father. And you, created *for* heaven.

But what does "heaven" mean when it comes to adoring God? Is it kneeling forever before God while repeating "Hosanna"? And, be honest with yourself, does that sound "heavenly" to you?

That's it? *Forever?*

What about the "beatific vision"? Another description. Eternity ... looking at God?

The *Catechism of the Catholic Church* offers a more detailed description:

This perfect life with the Most Holy Trinity — this communion of life and love with the Trinity, with the Virgin Mary, the angels and all the blessed — is called "heaven." Heaven is the ultimate end and fulfillment of the deepest human longings, the state of supreme, definitive happiness.

To live in heaven is "to be with Christ." (CCC 1024–1025)

Why bring that up here, at the beginning of a book on adoration? Because it can be easy, especially in the early stages of this form of devotion, to think of it as just kneeling before a tabernacle or monstrance. Just staring at the receptacle holding Our Lord in the Eucharist. Just watching the minutes slowly pass.

St. Faustina says, "Not so." Yes, she knelt. Yes, no doubt, she stared. Yes, time passed but … too quickly.

The young nun was living "in heaven," in that Polish convent. In that chapel or on her sick bed when she made a "spiritual adoration." It was there that she adored Our Lord. It was there that she found, for a too-brief time each day, the Most Holy Trinity, Our Lady, the angels, and the saints.

What she describes in her diary is, literally, heaven on earth.

It's what God offers you. What He offers to share with you.

Probably not visions and voices, but graces and blessings. Sometimes wordless nudges or startling insights. Certainly joy. And peace. A bit of heaven on earth for you. You and God, together.

And it could be that when the time comes for you to leave earth, to enter heaven, it will be a gentle transition. It will be a familiar "place" — or rather, state of being — because you've visited it before, time and again. Or more accurately, God brought it when He visited with you, time and again.

How do you get closer to that ideal in your own acts of adoration? The same way you move forward in ordinary tasks or in virtue. No miracles. Just practice, perseverance, patience, and prayer.

And just as there are others who have gone before you, who can help you with life in general — parents, teachers, mentors, and so on — those who have become more proficient at adoration want the same for you.

St. Faustina wants the same for you. That's what this book is about. Yes, it includes her extraordinary experiences, but also her advice and example.

Just how central was adoration to her life as a religious? It was her life. Period.

Young Helena Kowalska was given the religious name Sister Maria Faustina. But years later, God may have tipped His hand just a bit when He called her to add "of the Most Blessed Sacrament."

She was His. And He was hers. Eternally.

———

You've been on my mind as I wrote this book. As I made my own visits of adoration before Our Lord in the Blessed Sacrament. As I researched, learned about — and marveled at — St. Faustina's growing closer and closer to Jesus. At her becoming more and more like Him.

During my visits, the beauty, power, and grace of adoration became clearer to me. With that, a deeper realization that God is truly there, in the Eucharist.

And as I wrote this book, as I spent time in adoration, you, your loved ones, and the souls of your dearly departed have been in my prayers.

Please pray for me and mine.

St. Faustina, pray for all of us. St. Faustina, pray *with* each of us. Amen.

— SUSAN

May You, Like Faustina, Find a Friend and Constant Companion in Jesus

Susan Tassone — longtime friend of the Marian Fathers of the Immaculate Conception — has a well-deserved reputation as the "Purgatory Lady." Few other Catholics working in the vineyard of the Lord today have spent as much time championing the cause of the holy souls. That's why I'm honored and delighted to write the foreword to her latest book.

Here are the many different elements of St. Faustina's adoration of Our Lord, both before the Eucharist in the chapel and privately in her room. That deep life-changing and soul-changing devotion was at the heart of her spirituality, personal life, and mission. They were acts partly for her own sake; partly for the sake of the world, so badly in need of Divine Mercy; and partly in response to the longing of Jesus' Sacred Heart for us to return His love.

Susan does a fabulous job of making this important aspect of the life of St. Faustina alive for us today. In fact, be sure to read her chapter on silent adoration. I find this one to be particularly practical. So many times people ask me, "Father, I don't know what to say in adoration." Well, sometimes the answer is simply say nothing. Let God do the talking!

Here's a book that can help you to pray with or without words. It's one to be used before Our Lord in the Blessed Sacrament *and* with Him at home.

I pray that you, like St. Faustina, draw tremendous spiritual benefits from your time in adoration. And, as Susan recommends, that you include prayers for the holy souls in purgatory as you visit with our Crucified Lord, the willing Victim. May you, like St. Faustina, find a friend and constant companion in Him, as you make adoration a normal — and central — part of your own life.

May God bless you, may Mary Immaculate always intercede for you, and may St. Faustina pray for you.

— FATHER CHRIS M. ALAR, M.I.C.
Director, Association of Marian Helpers
National Shrine of The Divine Mercy
Stockbridge, Massachusetts

INTRODUCTION

Praying Fervently, Gazing Radiantly

Look to him, and be radiant.
— PSALM 34:5

Once, the *[Divine Mercy]* image was being exhibited over the altar during the Corpus Christi procession.... When the priest exposed the Blessed Sacrament, and the choir began to sing, the rays from the image pierced the Sacred Host and spread out all over the world. Then I heard these words: These rays of mercy will pass through you, just as they have passed through this Host, and they will go out through all the world. At these words, profound joy invaded my soul. (441)

Adoration has been a central Catholic devotion for centuries, beloved by saints, popes, and countless devout men, women, and children.

Among them was St. Faustina — who added "of the Blessed Sacrament" to her religious name:

One hour spent at the foot of the altar in the greatest dryness of spirit is dearer to me than a hundred years of worldly pleasure. (254)

Striving to be in constant union with Jesus, she visited the Blessed Sacrament throughout her day as much and often as possible, sometimes if only to quickly genuflect at the chapel's door as she passed by, smiling to Our Lord.

———

What Did St. Faustina Learn in Front of the Blessed Sacrament?

There's a Polish proverb that goes: *Z kim się zadajesz takim się stajesz* — "You become the one you befriend."

When St. Faustina knelt in front of the tabernacle, she prayed fervently, gazing radiantly at the altar. Jesus in the Eucharist was to her a living person with whom she wanted to talk at every moment. All the basic forms of prayer — adoration, petition, intercession, and thanksgiving — were part of those visits.

I wrote this book to help you, and encourage you, to pray and adore with St. Faustina. She wept in front of Our Lord in the Eucharist, interceded for others, shared her joys with Him, and acknowledged her weaknesses. She obtained self-knowledge, asked for healing, adored, loved, listened, thanked, and rested in Him.

As St. Faustina's soul united with Jesus, the fruit of her adoration was an image of Divine Mercy and a deeper and deeper relationship with the living Host. It gave her nourishment to confront her many challenges, as from that source sprang a fountain of love for all.

St. Faustina had a peace that radiated to all. She offered faith, hope, and charity — and love, compassion, and healing, as she went about doing good, as she left the chapel and went back to the world, herself becoming a "living host."

> *[Jesus said to her:]* "I delight in you as in a living host; let nothing terrify you; I am with you." (923)

St. Faustina immersed herself in the fire of His love and the abyss of His mercy, and she came to know herself and her God. It was adoration that called her forth to go out and help others, and adoration empowered her to share Jesus' compassion to everyone she encountered.

Jesus was her teacher. He taught her to treat trials as a positive opportunity to learn love of neighbor. She had grudges but she took them to Jesus, and He erased the memory from her soul, transforming it into overwhelming kindness and concern for others. Simply put, He taught her not to judge others.

This is how she became holy, how she became a saint.

What Can You Learn by Adoration?

Just as He patiently waited for St. Faustina, Our Lord in the Blessed Sacrament waits for you. Just as she grew more like Him, so can you. You can become a "living host." You can come to better know yourself and your God, and apply that knowledge, that truth, in all facets of your life.

You can become a saint.

What Is Adoration?

Here's how the *Catechism* explains it:

Adoration is the first attitude of man acknowledging that he is a creature before his Creator. It exalts the greatness of the Lord who made us and the almighty power of the Savior who sets us free from evil. Adoration is homage of the spirit to the "King of Glory," respectful silence in the presence of the "ever greater" God. Adoration of the thrice-holy and sovereign God of love blends with humility and gives assurance to our supplications. (CCC 2628)

What Is Eucharistic Adoration?

Again to the *Catechism*:

> It is highly fitting that Christ should have wanted to remain present to his Church in this unique way. Since Christ was about to take his departure from his own in his visible form, he wanted to give us his sacramental presence; since he was about to offer himself on the cross to save us, he wanted us to have the memorial of the love with which he loved us "to the end," even to the giving of his life. In his Eucharistic presence he remains mysteriously in our midst as the one who loved us and gave himself up for us, and he remains under signs that express and communicate this love:
>
>> The Church and the world have a great need for Eucharistic worship. Jesus awaits us in this sacrament of love. Let us not refuse the time to go to meet him in adoration, in contemplation full of faith, and open to making amends for the serious offenses and crimes of the world. Let our adoration never cease. (CCC 1380, quoting St. John Paul II's apostolic letter *Dominicae Cenae*, on the mystery and worship of the Eucharist)

How Is *St. Faustina Prayer Book for Adoration* Designed to Help You Adore God?

Like St. Faustina, sometimes you'll be able to adore God before the Blessed Sacrament and, at other times, at home or another place when you're unable to visit a church or chapel.

How did Faustina do it? That's what her diary is all about. It's what this book is all about. Here you'll find the themes, the devotions, and the prayers that she returned to time and again.

In the sections of this prayer book, let St. Faustina draw you nearer to the Lord in the Real Presence with her reflections and prayers. In several chapters, she surrounds you with Mary, the angels, the saints, and the holy souls, as you come before the tabernacle in adoration. In other sections, St. Faustina models for your spiritual adoration at home, private devotion after Communion, and the powerful prayer of silence. And in still other places, she leads you to the cross and helps you to worship the Crucified Lord.

Let this wonderful saint be your spiritual companion in your times of adoration.

I. Adoration of Jesus in the Blessed Sacrament

My soul thirsts for God,
for the living God.
When shall I come and behold
the face of God?
— PSALM 42:2

For now we see in a mirror dimly, but then face to face.
— 1 CORINTHIANS 13:12

Gazing on Jesus with St. Faustina

St. Faustina's description of one part of her time spent in adoration shows a relationship with Christ that was profoundly simple but deeply intimate. It was the look — the gaze — of love.

Some six decades after her death in 1938, the *Catechism of the Catholic Church* named and explained that way of "looking": "Contemplation is a *gaze* of faith, fixed on Jesus" (CCC 2715, emphasis in original).

"I LOOK AT HIM AND HE LOOKS AT ME"

"This is what a certain peasant of Ars in the time of his holy curé [St. John Vianney] used to say while praying before the tabernacle. This focus on Jesus is a renunciation of self. His gaze purifies our heart; the light of the countenance of Jesus illumines the eyes of our heart and teaches us to see everything in the light of his truth and his compassion for all men. Contemplation also turns its gaze on the mysteries of the life of Christ. Thus it learns the 'interior knowledge of our Lord,' the more to love him and follow him." (CCC 2715)

Once Jesus said to me, My gaze from this *[Divine Mercy]* image is like My gaze from the cross. (326)

Now I see only dimly, Lord, but because of Your Divine Mercy the time will come when I see you face-to-face.

From the very first time that I came to know the Lord, the gaze of my soul became drowned in Him for all eternity. Each time the Lord draws close to me and my knowledge of Him grows deeper, a more perfect love grows within my soul. (231)

Now I see only dimly, Lord, but because of Your Divine Mercy the time will come when I see you face-to-face.

O my Jesus, delight of my heart, You know my desires.... I want to live beneath Your divine gaze, for You alone are enough for me. (306)

Now I see only dimly, Lord, but because of Your Divine Mercy the time will come when I see you face-to-face.

At that very moment, I felt some kind of fire in my heart. I feel my senses deadening and have no idea of what is going on around me. I feel the Lord's gaze piercing me through and through. I am very much aware of His greatness and my misery. (432)

Now I see only dimly, Lord, but because of Your Divine Mercy the time will come when I see you face-to-face.

Jesus, my Love, today gave me to understand how much He loves me, although there is such an enormous gap between us, the Creator and the creature; and yet, in a way, there is something like equality: love fills up the gap. He Himself descends to me and makes me capable of communing with Him. I immerse myself in Him, losing myself as it were; and yet, under His loving gaze, my soul gains strength and power and an awareness that it loves and is especially loved. It knows that the Mighty One protects it. Such prayer, though short, benefits the soul greatly, and whole hours of ordinary prayer do not give the soul that light which is given by a brief moment of this higher form of prayer. (815)

Now I see only dimly, Lord, but because of Your Divine Mercy the time will come when I see you face-to-face.

During a Forty Hours Devotion I saw the face of the Lord Jesus in the Sacred Host which was exposed in the monstrance. Jesus was looking with kindness at everyone. (433)

Dearest Jesus, look with kindness on me. Have mercy on me as I look at the One whom, by my sins, I have pierced. And when You look at me, love me, and say, "Come, follow me," help me answer, "Yes. Yes. Yes." Right here, right now, Dearest Lord, let me gaze on You with my simple love and adoration, as You gaze on me with your infinite love and compassion.

Seeing the Hidden God Under the Fragile Form of Bread

"When I was seven years old," St. Faustina writes, "… before the Lord Jesus in the monstrance, the love of God was imparted to me for the first time and filled my little heart" (1404).

As she grew in wisdom and age and grace, that love deepened, but still Our Lord remained "hidden" in the Eucharist: "body, soul and divinity, under the fragile form of bread" (1718).

"Truly, thou art a God who hidest thyself, / O God of Israel, the Savior." (Is 45:15)

Later, she came to realize, to truly believe,

> When you unite Yourself with me in Communion, O God,
> I then feel my unspeakable greatness,
> A greatness which flows from You ...
> [W]ith Your help, I can become a saint. (1718)

> O Blessed Host, take up Your dwelling within my soul,
> O Thou my heart's purest love!
> With Your brilliance the darkness dispel.
> Refuse not Your grace to a humble heart.
> O Blessed Host, enchantment of all heaven,
> Though Your beauty be veiled
> And captured in a crumb of bread,
> Strong faith tears away that veil. (159)

At the feet of the Lord. Hidden Jesus, Eternal Love, our Source of Life, divine Madman, in that You forget Yourself and see only us. Before creating heaven and earth, You carried us in the depths of Your Heart. O Love, O depth of Your Abasement, O mystery of happiness, why do so few people know You? Why is Your love not returned? O Divine Love, why do You hide Your beauty? O infinite One beyond all understanding, the more I know You the less I comprehend You; but because I cannot comprehend You, I better comprehend Your greatness. I do not envy the Seraphim their fire, for I have a greater gift deposited in my heart. They admire you in rapture, but Your Blood mingles with mine. Love is heaven given us already here on earth. Oh, why do You hide in faith? Love tears away the veil. There is no veil before the eye of my soul, for You Yourself have drawn me into the bosom of secret love forever. Praise and glory be to You, O Indivisible Trinity, One God, unto ages of ages! (278)

O living Host, O hidden Jesus. You see the condition of my soul. Of myself, I am unable to utter Your Holy Name. I cannot bring forth from my heart the fire of love but, kneeling at Your feet, I cast upon the Tabernacle the gaze of my soul, a gaze of faithfulness. (1239)

"When I entered the chapel, I received an inner understanding of the great reward that God is preparing for us, not only for our good deeds, but also for our sincere desire to perform them. What a great grace of God this is!" (450)

My heart is drawn there where my God is hidden,
Where He dwells with us day and night,
Clothed in the White Host;
He governs the whole world, He communes with souls.

My heart is drawn there where my God is hiding,
Where His love is immolated.
But my heart senses that the living water is here;
It is my living God, though a veil hides Him. (1591)

Hidden Jesus, in You lies all my strength. From my most tender years, the Lord Jesus in the Blessed Sacrament has attracted me to Himself. Once, when I was seven years old, at a Vesper Service, conducted before the Lord Jesus in the monstrance, the love of God was imparted to me for the first time and filled my little heart; and the Lord gave me understanding of divine things. From that day until this, my love for the hidden God has been growing constantly to the point of closest intimacy. All the strength of my soul flows from the Blessed Sacrament. I spend all my free moments in conversation with Him. He is my Master. (1404)

To stay at Your feet, O hidden God,
Is the delight and paradise of my soul.
Here, You give me to know You, O incomprehensible One,
And You speak to me sweetly: Give Me, give Me your heart.

Silent conversation, alone with You,
Is to experience what heavenly beings enjoy,
And to say to God, "I will, I will give You my heart, O Lord,"
While You, O great and incomprehensible One, accept it graciously.

Love and sweetness are my soul's life,
And Your unceasing presence in my soul.
I live on earth in constant rapture,
And like a Seraph I repeat, "Hosanna!"

O You Who are hidden, body, soul and divinity,
Under the fragile form of bread,
You are my life from Whom springs an abundance of graces;
And, for me, You surpass the delights of heaven.

When you unite Yourself with me in Communion, O God,
I then feel my unspeakable greatness,
A greatness which flows from You, O Lord, I humbly confess,
And despite my misery, with Your help, I can become a saint. (1718)

Hidden Jesus, life of my soul,
Object of my ardent desire,

Nothing will stifle Your love in my heart.
The power of our mutual love assures me of that.

Hidden Jesus, glorious pledge of my resurrection,
All my life is concentrated in You.
It is You, O Host, who empower me to love forever,
And I know that You will love me as Your child in return.

Hidden Jesus, my purest love,
My life with You has begun already here on earth,
And it will become fully manifest in the eternity to come,
Because our mutual love will never change.

Hidden Jesus, sole desire of my soul,
You alone are to me more than the delights of heaven.
My soul searches for You only, who are above all gifts and graces,
You who come to me under the form of bread.

Hidden Jesus, take at last to Yourself my thirsting heart
Which burns for You with the pure fire of the Seraphim.
I go through life in Your footsteps, invincible,
With head held high, like a knight, feeble maid though I be. (1427)

My Lord and my God, "hidden" in the Eucharist, I want to use the faith you've given me, the grace with which you've blessed me, and the love with which you've filled my own "little heart," to "tear away the veil" and to realize, to truly believe, that with your help, I, too, can become the person — can become the saint — you're calling me to be.

II. Adoration with the Holy Spirit and the Holy Trinity

*The Spirit helps us in our weakness; for we do not
know how to pray as we ought, but the Spirit himself intercedes for us with sighs too deep for words.*
— ROMANS 8:26

Prayers of Adoration to the Holy Spirit

St. Faustina understood that the Divine Spirit — the Holy Spirit — works within each one of us to make us holy. To fill our life and our soul with His fruits and gifts. To lead us to sainthood.

Setting an example for all of us, in the midst of busy work periods she would often pause for a moment and pray: "Most Holy Trinity, I adore you!"

In her profound prayer "O Divine Spirit," she invites us to welcome the Holy Spirit into our hearts under all circumstances and allow Him to penetrate our souls and introduce us into the life of the Holy Trinity.

O Divine Spirit

O Divine Spirit, Spirit of truth and of light,
Dwell ever in my soul by Your divine grace.
May Your breath dissipate the darkness,
And in this light may good deeds be multiplied.

O Divine Spirit, Spirit of love and of mercy,
You pour the balm of trust into my heart,
Your grace confirms my soul in good,
Giving it the invincible power of constancy.

O Divine Spirit, Spirit of peace and of joy,
You invigorate my thirsting heart
And pour into it the living fountain of God's love,
Making it intrepid for battle.

O Divine Spirit, my soul's most welcome guest,
For my part, I want to remain faithful to You;
Both in days of joy and in the agony of suffering,
I want always, O Spirit of God, to live in Your presence.

O Divine Spirit, who pervade my whole being
And give me to know Your Divine, Triune Life,
And lead me into the mystery of Your Divine Being,
Initiating me into Your Divine Essence,
Thus united to You, I will live a life without end. (1411)

Prayers of Adoration to the Holy Trinity

When St. Faustina asked the Holy Trinity, "Who are You?," this was God's response:

On one occasion I was reflecting on the Holy Trinity, on the essence of God. I absolutely wanted to know and fathom who God is…. In an instant my spirit was caught up into what seemed to be the next world. I saw an inaccessible light, and in this light what appeared like three sources of light which I could not understand. And out of that light came words in the form of lightning which encircled heaven and earth. Not understanding anything, I was very sad. Suddenly, from this sea of inaccessible light came our dearly beloved Savior, unutterably beautiful with His shining Wounds. And from this light came a voice which said, Who God is in His Essence, no one will fathom, neither the mind of Angels nor of man. Jesus said to me, Get to know God by contemplating His attributes. (30)

The first attribute which the Lord gave me to know is His holiness. His holiness is so great that all the Powers and Virtues tremble before Him. The pure spirits veil their faces and lose themselves in unending adoration, and with one single word they express the highest form of adoration; that is — Holy.... The holiness of God is poured out upon the Church of God and upon every living soul in it, but not in the same degree. There are souls who are completely penetrated by God, and there are those who are barely alive.

The second kind of knowledge which the Lord granted me concerns His justice. His justice is so great and penetrating that it reaches deep into the heart of things, and all things stand before Him in naked truth, and nothing can withstand Him.

The third attribute is love and mercy. And I understood that the greatest attribute is love and mercy. It unites the creature with the Creator. This immense love and abyss of mercy are made known in the Incarnation of the Word and in the Redemption [of humanity], and it is here that I saw this as the greatest of all God's attributes. (180)

Most Holy Trinity, I trust in Your infinite mercy. God is my Father and so I, His child, have every claim to His divine Heart; and the greater the darkness, the more complete our trust should be. (357)

O Holy Trinity, in whom is contained the inner life of God, the Father, the Son, and the Holy Spirit, eternal joy, inconceivable depth of love, poured out upon all creatures and constituting their happiness, honor and glory be to Your holy name forever and ever. Amen. (525)

Holy Trinity, One God, incomprehensible in the greatness of Your mercy for creatures, and especially for poor sinners, You have made known the abyss of Your mercy, incomprehensible and unfathomable [as it is] to any mind, whether of man or angel. Our nothingness and our misery are drowned in Your greatness. O infinite goodness, who can ever praise You sufficiently? Can there be found a soul that understands You in Your love? O Jesus, there are such souls, but they are few. (361)

O Holy Trinity, Eternal God, my spirit is drowned in Your beauty. The ages are as nothing in Your sight. You are always the same. Oh, how great is Your majesty. (576)

O Holy Trinity, Eternal God, I want to shine in the crown of Your mercy as a tiny gem whose beauty depends on the ray of Your light and of Your inscrutable mercy. All that is beautiful in my soul is Yours, O God; of myself, I am ever nothing. (617)

Be adored, O Most Holy Trinity, now and for all time. Be adored in all Your works and all Your creatures. May the greatness of Your mercy be admired and glorified, O God. (5)

III. Adoration with Mary, the Perfect Adorer

"My soul magnifies the Lord,
and my spirit rejoices in God my Savior."
— LUKE 1:46-47

Like Our Lady, St. Faustina's soul magnified the Lord, and her spirit rejoiced in God, her Savior.

Like Our Lady, she, too, experienced deep personal sorrows.

And like Our Lady, she adored Jesus. One, in the twentieth century, kneeling before the tabernacle. The other, in the first century, chosen by God to be that first tabernacle.

Of course, the two women were such dear and intimate friends. Not just lifelong, but for all eternity.

In order to fulfill God's will, Faustina knew to stay very close to Our Lady. She loved the Rosary, the Immaculate Heart, Marian Novenas, the sorrows of Our Lady, and consecration prayers to the Mother of God. She consecrated to Our Lady all her concerns. Faustina understood that without the Blessed Mother, there would be no Eucharistic Jesus. In order to love Jesus in the Eucharist we must love His Mother, the first tabernacle.

I Model My Life on You

O sweet Mother of God,
I model my life on You;
You are for me the bright dawn;
In You I lose myself, enraptured.

O Mother, Immaculate Virgin,
In You the divine ray is reflected,
Midst storms, 'tis You who teach me to love the Lord,
O my shield and defense from the foe. (1232)

"In the evening, when I was praying, the Mother of God told me, Your lives must be like Mine: quiet and hidden, in unceasing union with God, pleading for humanity and preparing the world for the second coming of God." (625)

Mary's Song of Adoration: The Magnificat

My soul magnifies the Lord,
and my spirit rejoices in God my Savior,
for he has regarded the low estate of his handmaiden.
For behold, henceforth all generations will call me blessed;
for he who is mighty has done great things for me,
and holy is his name.
And his mercy is on those who fear him
from generation to generation.
He has shown strength with his arm,
he has scattered the proud in the imagination of their hearts,
he has put down the mighty from their thrones,
and exalted those of low degree;
he has filled the hungry with good things,
and the rich he has sent empty away.
He has helped his servant Israel,
in remembrance of his mercy,

as he spoke to our fathers,
to Abraham and to his posterity for ever. (Lk 1:46–55)

A Rosary of Adoration

St. Faustina loved to pray the Rosary, not just in the chapel but while walking or even while weeding the garden! She encouraged the "wards" under her supervision to pray the Rosary — or say Hail Marys — for someone living or dead.

The funeral of Sister Faustina — who died on October 5, 1938 — took place two days later on the First Friday of the month and the feast of Our Lady of the Rosary.

> "Christmas Eve. Today I was closely united with the Mother of God. I relived her interior sentiments. In the evening, before the ceremony of the breaking of the wafer, I went into the chapel to break the wafer, in spirit, with my loved ones, and I asked the Mother of God for graces for them. My spirit was totally steeped in God." (182)

The Joyful Mysteries

1. The Annunciation of the Angel Gabriel to Mary

The Lord is with me. Here and now. I praise You, God. I bless You. I adore You. I glorify You. I give You thanks for Your great glory.

2. The Visitation of Mary to Elizabeth

And how does this happen that you, my God, should come to me? I praise You, God. I bless You. I adore You. I glorify You. I give You thanks for Your great glory.

3. The Nativity of Jesus in Bethlehem

Glory to God in the highest! God calls me to kneel before His beloved Son. I praise you, God. I bless you. I adore you. I glorify you. I give you thanks for your great glory.

4. The Presentation of Jesus in the Temple

God has let my eyes see His salvation. I praise You, God. I bless You. I adore You. I glorify You. I give You thanks for Your great glory.

5. The Finding of Jesus in the Temple

What — and — who am I looking for? Did I not know I can always find Him in His Father's house? I praise You, God. I bless You. I adore You. I glorify You. I give You thanks for Your great glory.

The Luminous Mysteries
1. The Baptism of Jesus in the River Jordan

Thank you, Heavenly Father, that I, too, am Your beloved child. I praise You, God. I bless You. I adore You. I glorify You. I give You thanks for Your great glory.

2. The Wedding Feast at Cana

Through the intercession of Mary, there are miracles in my life. I praise You, God. I bless You. I adore You. I glorify You. I give You thanks for Your great glory.

3. The Proclamation of the Kingdom of God

Like the early disciples, I am sent to share the Good News. I praise You, God. I bless You. I adore You. I glorify You. I give You thanks for Your great glory.

4. The Transfiguration of Jesus

True God of true God, You call me to see You and serve You. I praise You, God. I bless You. I adore You. I glorify You. I give You thanks for Your great glory.

5. The Institution of the Eucharist

My Lord and my God, I take and eat! I praise You, God. I bless You. I adore You. I glorify You. I give You thanks for Your great glory.

The Sorrowful Mysteries

1. The Agony in the Garden

Not my will, Father, but Yours be done. I praise You, God. I bless You. I adore You. I glorify You. I give You thanks for Your great glory.

2. The Scourging at the Pillar

What have I done to You, dear Jesus? What have I done? I praise You, God. I bless You. I adore You. I glorify You. I give You thanks for Your great glory.

3. The Crowning with Thorns

Christ, my king, Christ, my prince of peace. I praise You, God. I bless You. I adore You. I glorify You. I give You thanks for Your great glory.

4. The Carrying of the Cross

Step by step, You never leave my side, dear Lord. I praise You, God. I bless You. I adore You. I glorify You. I give You thanks for Your great glory.

5. The Crucifixion

My God, my God, You never forsake me. I praise You, God. I bless You. I adore You. I glorify You. I give You thanks for Your great glory.

The Glorious Mysteries

1. The Resurrection

On the third day, You rose from the dead. Today You are with me. I praise You, God. I bless You. I adore You. I glorify You. I give You thanks for Your great glory.

2. The Ascension

You did not leave me an orphan; You have come to me. I praise You, God. I bless You. I adore You. I glorify You. I give You thanks for Your great glory.

3. The Descent of the Holy Spirit

Baptized with the Holy Spirit and fire, I am Yours. I praise You, God. I bless You. I adore You. I glorify You. I give You thanks for Your great glory.

4. The Assumption of Mary

I believe in the resurrection of the body. I believe in life everlasting. I praise You, God. I bless You. I adore You. I glorify You. I give You thanks for Your great glory.

5. The Coronation of Mary

Queen of Heaven, Mother of God, help me do whatever Jesus tells me. I praise You, God. I bless You. I adore You. I glorify You. I give You thanks for Your great glory.

The Dolors of Our Lady

Reflect on the sorrows that afflicted Mary's heart as an act of adoration.

—

O God, come to my assistance; O Lord, make haste to help me. Glory be...

I grieve for you, O Mary most sorrowful, in the affliction of your tender heart at the prophecy of the holy and aged Simeon. Dear Mother, by your heart so afflicted, obtain for me the virtue of humility and the gift of the holy fear of God. Hail Mary ...

I grieve for you, O Mary most sorrowful, in the anguish of your most affectionate heart during the flight into Egypt and your sojourn there. Dear Mother, by your heart so troubled, obtain for me the virtue of generosity, especially toward the poor, and the gift of piety. Hail Mary ...

I grieve for you, O Mary most sorrowful, in those anxieties which tried your troubled heart at the loss of your dear Jesus. Dear Mother, by your heart so full of anguish, obtain for me the virtue of chastity and the gift of knowledge. Hail Mary …

I grieve for you, O Mary most sorrowful, in the consternation of your heart at meeting Jesus as He carried His cross. Dear Mother, by your heart so troubled, obtain for me the virtue of patience and the gift of fortitude. Hail Mary …

I grieve for you, O Mary most sorrowful, in the martyrdom which your generous heart endured in standing near Jesus in His agony. Dear Mother, by your afflicted heart, obtain for me the virtue of temperance and the gift of counsel. Hail Mary …

I grieve for you, O Mary most sorrowful, in the wounding of your compassionate heart, when the side of Jesus was struck by the lance before His body was removed from the cross. Dear Mother, by your heart thus transfixed, obtain for me the virtue of fraternal charity and the gift of understanding. Hail Mary …

I grieve for you, O Mary most sorrowful, for the pangs that wrenched your most loving heart at the burial of Jesus. Dear Mother, by your heart sunk in the bitterness of desolation, obtain for me the virtue of diligence and the gift of wisdom. Hail Mary …

"After the Power of the Father, the Wisdom of the Son, and the Tender Mercy of the Holy Spirit, nothing compares to the Power, Wisdom, and Tender Mercy of Mary."
— REVELATION TO ST. GERTRUDE

Let intercession be made for us, we beg You, O Lord Jesus Christ, now and at the hour of our death, before the throne of Your mercy, by the Blessed Virgin Mary, Your Mother, whose most holy soul was pierced by a sword of sorrow in the hour of Your bitter Passion. Through You, O Jesus Christ, Savior of the world, who, with the Father and the Holy Spirit, lives and reigns, world without end. Amen.

Act of Reparation to the Immaculate Heart of Mary

O Most Holy Virgin Mother, we listen with grief to the complaints of your Immaculate Heart surrounded with the thorns placed therein at every moment by the blasphemies and ingratitude of ungrateful humanity. We are moved by the ardent desire of loving you as Our Mother and of promoting a true devotion to your Immaculate Heart.

We therefore kneel before you to manifest the sorrow we feel for the grief that people cause you, and to atone by our prayers and sacrifices for the offenses with which they return your love. Obtain for them and for us the pardon of so many sins. Hasten the conversion of sinners that they may love Jesus and cease to offend the Lord, already so much offended. Turn your eyes of mercy toward us, that we may love God with all our heart on earth and enjoy Him forever in heaven. Amen.

> "Another time I heard *[Jesus say]* these words, Go to the Superior and ask her to allow you to make a daily hour of adoration for nine days. During this adoration try to unite yourself in prayer with My Mother. Pray with all your heart in union with Mary, and try also during this time to make the Way of the Cross." (32)

A Novena to Our Lady of the Most Blessed Sacrament

First Day: Our Lady of the Most Blessed Sacrament

Son of Mary and Son of God, body and blood, soul and divinity, present in the Most Blessed Sacrament, I adore you.

Holy Mary, Mother of God, pray for me, now and at the hour of my death.

Beloved Queen of Heaven, my Savior's first "tabernacle," help me more deeply and reverently ponder, appreciate, and adore who is in the tabernacle, in the monstrance, and in my own heart and soul. Jesus and Mary, today I pray for [mention your intention here].

Our Lady of the Most Blessed Sacrament, pray for me.

Help me, Dear Mother, do what Jesus tells me to do.

Second Day: Our Lady of the Most Holy Sacrifice of the Mass

Son of Mary and Son of God, body and blood, soul and divinity, present in the Most Blessed Sacrament, I adore you.

Holy Mary, Mother of God, pray for me, now and at the hour of my death.

Beloved Queen of Heaven, thank you for the sacrifices you made for me, including witnessing the death of your Son on the cross. Jesus and Mary, today I pray for [mention your intention here].

Our Lady of the Most Holy Sacrifice of the Mass, pray for me.

Help me, Dear Mother, do what Jesus tells me to do.

Third Day: Our Lady of Holy Communion

Son of Mary and Son of God, body and blood, soul and divinity, present in the Most Blessed Sacrament, I adore you.

Holy Mary, Mother of God, pray for me, now and at the hour of my death.

Beloved Queen of Heaven, thank you that your Son offers me the opportunity — the blessing, the grace — to "take and eat." Jesus and Mary, today I pray for [mention your intention here].

Our Lady of Holy Communion, pray for me.

Help me, Dear Mother, do what Jesus tells me to do.

Fourth Day: Our Lady of the Real Presence

Son of Mary and Son of God, body and blood, soul and divinity, present in the Most Blessed Sacrament, I adore you.

Holy Mary, Mother of God, pray for me, now and at the hour of my death.

Queen of Heaven, thank you that just as Our Lord was present in your womb, in the stable in Bethlehem, in your home in Nazareth, in the Temple, and in the towns and villages of Galilee and Judea, He's present in the Eucharist today. It is His Body. It is His Blood. Jesus and Mary, today I pray for [mention your intention here].

Our Lady of the Real Presence, pray for me.

Help me, Dear Mother, do what Jesus tells me to do.

Fifth Day: Our Lady, Model of Adorers

Son of Mary and Son of God, body and blood, soul and divinity, present in the Most Blessed Sacrament, I adore you.

Holy Mary, Mother of God, pray for me, now and at the hour of my death.

Beloved Queen of Heaven, help me look on your Son as you did on that night in Bethlehem, with wonder, awe, and thanksgiving. Help me see Him as you did at the foot of the cross, giving His life for me. Help me see Him as you do now, the Resurrected Lord, the Prince of Peace, Christ the King. Jesus and Mary, today I pray for [mention your intention here].

Our Lady, Model of Adorers, pray for me.

Help me, Dear Mother, do what Jesus tells me to do.

Sixth Day: Our Lady, Image of Thanksgiving

Son of Mary and Son of God, body and blood, soul and divinity, present in the Most Blessed Sacrament, I adore you.

Holy Mary, Mother of God, pray for me, now and at the hour of my death.

Beloved Queen of Heaven — Immaculate, Loving, Grateful Heart — help me better live my life as you lived yours, so gratefully and graciously. Jesus and Mary, today I pray for [mention your intention here].

Our Lady, Image of Thanksgiving, pray for me.

Help me, Dear Mother, do what Jesus tells me to do.

Seventh Day: Our Lady, Icon of Reparation

Son of Mary and Son of God, body and blood, soul and divinity, present in the Most Blessed Sacrament, I adore you.

Holy Mary, Mother of God, pray for me, now and at the hour of my death.

Beloved Queen of Heaven, you were the bridge between heaven and earth. You were the one who suffered through His passion and death as only a mother could. You were, you are, the one the Father chose to help me turn, to return, to Divine Mercy when I stumble. Jesus and Mary, today I pray for [mention your intention here].

Our Lady, Icon of Reparation, pray for me.

Help me, Dear Mother, do what Jesus tells me to do.

Eighth Day: Our Lady, Vessel of Prayer

Son of Mary and Son of God, body and blood, soul and divinity, present in the Most Blessed Sacrament, I adore you.

Holy Mary, Mother of God, pray for me, now and at the hour of my death.

Beloved Queen of Heaven, every word you spoke to your Son was a form of prayer, addressing the Second Person of the Blessed Trinity. Help me be more aware of His presence throughout my day. Help me never hesitate to tell Him what's in my heart or on my mind. Help spend quiet time with Him, sharing a silence that speaks deeply of our love. Jesus and Mary, today I pray for [mention your intention here].

Our Lady, Vessel of Prayer, pray for me.

Help me, Dear Mother, do what Jesus tells me to do.

Ninth Day: Our Lady, Dispenser of Eucharistic Graces

Son of Mary and Son of God, body and blood, soul and divinity, present in the Most Blessed Sacrament, I adore you.

Holy Mary, Mother of God, pray for me, now and at the hour of my death.

Queen of Heaven — not just full of grace but truly overflowing with it — help me be more open to the graces your Son stands ready to pour into my heart, my mind, and my soul. Help me use those graces generously in service to others, and so, in service to Him. Jesus and Mary, today I pray for [mention your intention here].

Our Lady, Dispenser of Eucharistic Graces, pray for me.

Help me, Dear Mother, do what Jesus tells me to do.

Concluding Prayer

Dearest Lady of the Most Blessed Sacrament, who am I that my Lord should come to me? As you did during your time on earth, help me lead others to Christ by what I say and especially by what I do.

Mary, Immaculate Virgin, take me under Your special protection and guard the purity of my soul, heart and body. You are the model and star of my life. (874)

IV. Adoration of the Crucified Jesus

"Father, if thou art willing, remove this cup from me;
nevertheless not my will, but thine, be done."
— LUKE 22:42

"Father, the hour has come; glorify thy Son
that the Son may glorify thee."
— JOHN 17:1

St. Faustina, St. John Paul II, and the Stations of the Cross

It's no exaggeration that the Stations of the Cross were among St. Faustina's favorite devotions. She prayed it daily, and whenever possible she said the prayers lying face down on the chapel floor, with her arms outstretched, assuming the position of one crucified. She believed that posture best expressed the atoning and penitential character of the prayers.

Her diary shows that she had it on good authority — on Good Authority — that praying the Stations of the Cross greatly pleased Jesus.

The same was true for arguably St. Faustina's biggest fan ... on earth: St. John Paul II. Small wonder that praying the stations was so dear to him as well. Why that devotion and Divine Mercy were so central to his own prayer life were keys to his pontificate.

Then, too, both knew that praying these prayers was a powerful way to assist the souls in purgatory.

But while St. Faustina always used the traditional fourteen stations, on Good Friday 1991 then-Pope John Paul II introduced a similar but different

Way of the Cross that incorporated specific scenes from Scripture. It ends with a fifteenth station: Jesus rises from the dead.

———

[Jesus said to St. Faustina:] My daughter, try your best to make the Stations of the Cross in this hour, provided that your duties permit it; and if you are not able to make the Stations of the Cross, then at least step into the chapel for a moment and adore, in the Blessed Sacrament, My Heart, which is full of mercy; and should you be unable to step into the chapel, immerse yourself in prayer there where you happen to be, if only for a very brief instant. (1572)

[Jesus said to St. Faustina:] Today bring to Me all devout and faithful souls, and immerse them in the ocean of My mercy. These souls brought Me consolation on the Way of the Cross. They were that drop of consolation in the midst of an ocean of bitterness. (1214)

When I make the Way of the Cross, I am deeply moved at the twelfth station [Jesus dies on the cross]. Here I reflect on the omnipotence of God's mercy which passed through the Heart of Jesus. In this open wound of the Heart of Jesus I enclose all poor humans ... and those individuals whom I love, as often as I make the Way of the Cross. (1309)

The Adoration Stations of the Cross

1. Jesus Is Condemned to Death

V. *We adore You, O Christ, and we praise You.*
R. *Because by Your holy cross, You have redeemed the world.*

In the midst of all sufferings, both physical and spiritual, as well as in darkness and desolation, I will remain silent, like a dove, and not complain.

I will empty myself continually at His feet in order to obtain mercy for poor souls. (504)

Transform me, Lord Jesus, ever present in the Eucharist; in my heart, my mind, and my soul; and in my life. I pray for those who are persecuted, for those who are imprisoned, for those who have been condemned to death. Help them feel Your presence and Your peace. Blessed be Your name forever.

2. Jesus Is Made to Carry the Cross

V. We adore You, O Christ, and we praise You.
R. Because by Your holy cross, You have redeemed the world.

Once during an adoration, the Lord demanded that I give myself up to Him as an offering, by bearing a certain suffering in atonement, not only for the sins of the world in general, but specifically for transgressions committed in this house. (190)

Transform me, Lord Jesus, ever present in the Eucharist; in my heart, my mind, and my soul; and in my life. I pray that I'll have the courage and faith to accept whatever burdens and hardships I'm called to bear. Give me the wisdom to better understand that they are part of my own way of the cross, my own path home to You. Blessed be Your name forever.

3. Jesus Falls the First Time

V. We adore You, O Christ, and we praise You.
R. Because by Your holy cross, You have redeemed the world.

Jesus again gave me a few directives: First, do not fight against a temptation by yourself, but disclose it to the confessor at once, and then the temptation will lose all its force. Second, during these ordeals do not lose your peace; live in My presence; ask My Mother and the Saints for help. Third, have the certitude that I am looking at you and supporting you. Fourth, do not fear either struggles of the soul or any temptations, because I am supporting you; if only you are willing to fight, know that the victory is always on your side. Fifth, know that by fighting bravely you give Me great glory and amass merits for yourself. Temptation gives you a chance to show Me your fidelity. (1560)

Transform me, Lord Jesus, ever present in the Eucharist; in my heart, my mind, and my soul; and in my life. I ask Your forgiveness for when I have fallen, for when I have sinned. Give me the grace to come to You in the Sacrament of Reconciliation and, through the priest acting in the person of Christ, to hear Your words of forgiveness, healing, and hope. Blessed be Your name forever.

4. Jesus Meets His Blessed Mother

V. *We adore You, O Christ, and we praise You.*
R. *Because by Your holy cross, You have redeemed the world.*

I heard the voice of Our Lady: Know, my daughter, that although I was raised to the Dignity of Mother of God, seven swords of pain pierced my heart. (786)

Transform me, Lord Jesus, ever present in the Eucharist; in my heart, my mind, and my soul; and in my life. I am so sorry, dear Jesus, for the suffering my sins caused Your mother. That, because of me, You accepted Your way of the cross. Help me be patient, kind, and forgiving to those who cause me pain. Help me, like our dear Blessed Mother, magnify the love You have for each of us. Blessed be Your name forever.

5. Simon of Cyrene Helps Jesus Carry His Cross

V. *We adore You, O Christ, and we praise You.*
R. *Because by Your holy cross, You have redeemed the world.*

Once when I was being crushed by these dreadful sufferings, I went into the chapel and said from the bottom of my soul, "Do what You will with me, O Jesus, I will adore You in everything. May Your will be done in me, O my Lord and my God, and I will praise Your infinite mercy." Through this act of submission, these terrible torments left me. Suddenly I saw Jesus, who said to me, I am always in your heart. An inconceivable joy entered my soul, and a great love of God set my heart aflame. I see that God never tries us beyond what we are able to suffer. Oh, I fear nothing; if God sends such great suffering to a soul, He upholds it with an even greater grace, although we are not aware of it. One act of trust at such moments gives greater glory to God than whole hours passed in prayer filled with consolations. (78)

Transform me, Lord Jesus, ever present in the Eucharist; in my heart, my mind, and my soul; and in my life. Thank you, Jesus, for the "Simons" who have made such a difference in my life. Richly bless them. Help me be less hesitant to step forward to help those in need. Blessed be Your name forever.

6. Veronica Wipes the Face of Jesus

V. *We adore You, O Christ, and we praise You.*
R. *Because by Your holy cross, You have redeemed the world.*

Jesus, imprint upon my heart and soul Your own humility. I love You, Jesus, to the point of madness, You who were crushed with suffering as described by the prophet [cf. Isaiah 53:2–9], as if he could not see the human form in You because of Your great suffering. It is in this condition, Jesus, that I love You to the point of madness. O eternal and infinite God, what has love done to You? (267)

O Jesus, hidden God,
My heart perceives You
Though veils hide You;
You know that I love You. (524)

Transform me, Lord Jesus, ever present in the Eucharist; in my heart, my mind, and my soul; and in my life. You have said my helping "the least" among us is helping You, but sometimes I choose not to offer them — to offer You — comfort. You have said I am to love my enemies and pray for them, but sometimes I show no love to them, I say no prayers for them. Sometimes what I fail to do keeps Your face hidden from me. Lord Jesus, cure my blindness. Blessed be Your name forever.

7. Jesus Falls the Second Time

V. We adore You, O Christ, and we praise You.
R. Because by Your holy cross, You have redeemed the world.

It so happened that I fell again into a certain error, in spite of a sincere resolution not to do so — even though the lapse was a minor imperfection and rather involuntary — and at this I felt such acute pain in my soul that I interrupted my work and went to the chapel for a while. Falling at the feet of Jesus, with love and a great deal of pain, I apologized to the Lord, all the more ashamed because of the fact that in my conversation with Him after Holy Communion this very morning I had promised to be faithful to Him. Then I heard these words: If it hadn't been for this small imperfection, you wouldn't have come to Me. Know that as often as you come to Me, humbling yourself and asking My forgiveness, I pour out a superabundance of graces on your soul, and your imperfection vanishes before My eyes, and I see only your love and your humility. You lose nothing but gain much. (1293)

Transform me, Lord Jesus, ever present in the Eucharist; in my heart, my mind, and my soul; and in my life. Time and again I have firmly resolved with the help of Your grace to sin no more, but I fall, Lord. I fail. Once again, I ask Your forgiveness and take great comfort in knowing that You will pour out a superabundance of graces on my soul, that my imperfection will vanish before Your eyes, and that You will see only my love and humility. Blessed be Your name forever.

8. Jesus Speaks to the Women of Jerusalem

V. We adore You, O Christ, and we praise You.
R. Because by Your holy cross, You have redeemed the world.

I am so taken up with His Passion that I cannot withhold my tears. I would like to hide somewhere in order to give myself freely to the sorrow which flows from the consideration of His Passion. (977)

Transform me, Lord Jesus, ever present in the Eucharist; in my heart, my mind, and my soul; and in my life. On Your way of the cross, You spoke to those who stood nearby weeping. Today, dear Jesus, You speak to me. Right here and right now, help me listen. Help me hear in my heart what You are saying to me. Blessed be Your name forever.

9. Jesus Falls the Third Time

V. We adore You, O Christ, and we praise You.
R. Because by Your holy cross, You have redeemed the world.

Soul *[striving after perfection]*: Lord, the reason for my sadness is that, in spite of my sincere resolutions, I fall again into the same faults. I make resolutions in the morning, but in the evenings I see how much I have departed from them.

Jesus: You see, My child, what you are of yourself. The cause of your falls is that you rely too much upon yourself and too little on Me. But let this not sadden you so much. You are dealing with the God of mercy, which your misery cannot exhaust. Remember, I did not allot only a certain number of pardons. (1488)

Transform me, Lord Jesus, ever present in the Eucharist; in my heart, my mind, and my soul; and in my life. Help me be more aware of Your presence when I foolishly try to rely on myself alone. Help me remember You are the all-loving God of infinite mercy when I stumble or fall. Pardon me, Jesus, for thinking You will not pardon me. Blessed be Your name forever.

10. Jesus Is Stripped of His Garments

V. We adore You, O Christ, and we praise You.
R. Because by Your holy cross, You have redeemed the world.

Jesus was suddenly standing before me, stripped of His clothes, His body completely covered with wounds, His eyes flooded with tears and blood, His face disfigured and covered with spittle. (268)

He said to me, It is in My Passion that you must seek light and strength. … I meditated on Jesus' terrible Passion, and I understood that what I was suffering was nothing compared to the Savior's Passion, and that even the smallest imperfection was the cause of this terrible suffering. Then my soul was filled with very great contrition. (654)

Transform me, Lord Jesus, ever present in the Eucharist; in my heart, my mind, and my soul; and in my life. There are times, Jesus, when I do not like to look closely at the crucifix. Times I do not like to closely read the words of the Evangelists when they speak of Your Passion. That is because if I do, when I do, I realize what I did to You. But, Lord Jesus, when I do look, when I do read, I also realize what You did for me. By Your cross and resurrection, You have set me free. Thank you, dear Jesus, thank you. Blessed be Your name forever.

11. Jesus Is Nailed to the Cross

V. *We adore You, O Christ, and we praise You.*
R. *Because by Your holy cross, You have redeemed the world.*

He who knows how to forgive prepares for himself many graces from God. As often as I look upon the cross, so often will I forgive with all my heart. (390)

Transform me, Lord Jesus, ever present in the Eucharist; in my heart, my mind, and my soul; and in my life. What You offer me is complete and eternal forgiveness. There is no sin that can keep me from You if I turn to You with a humble and contrite heart. Those hands, once nailed to the cross — those arms, once spread wide on that rough wood — are open now to welcome me into Your loving and merciful embrace. Blessed be Your name forever.

12. Jesus Dies on the Cross

V. We adore You, O Christ, and we praise You.
R. Because by Your holy cross, You have redeemed the world.

You expired, Jesus, but the source of life gushed forth for souls, and the ocean of mercy opened up for the whole world. O Fount of Life, unfathomable Divine Mercy, envelop the whole world and empty Yourself out upon us. (1319)

Transform me, Lord Jesus, ever present in the Eucharist; in my heart, my mind, and my soul; and in my life. You emptied yourself for me, dear Jesus. When I feel empty, fill me with Your presence. Fill me with Your love. Blessed be Your name forever.

13. Jesus Is Taken Down from the Cross

V. We adore You, O Christ, and we praise You.
R. Because by Your holy cross, You have redeemed the world.

Mother of God, Your soul was plunged into a sea of bitterness; look upon Your child and teach her to suffer and to love while suffering. Fortify my soul that pain will not break it. Mother of grace, teach me to live by [the power of] God. (315)

Transform me, Lord Jesus, ever present in the Eucharist; in my heart, my mind, and my soul; and in my life. In the eyes of the world, You looked like a complete failure, dear Jesus. Sometimes, when I look at my life, that's how I feel. But if, like You, I do the Father's will for me — no matter where it takes me, no matter what it asks of me — then I will shine as His beloved and faithful child. Blessed be Your name forever.

14. Jesus Is Placed in the Tomb

V. We adore You, O Christ, and we praise You.
R. Because by Your holy cross, You have redeemed the world.

When I received Holy Communion, I said to Him, "Jesus, I thought about You so many times last night," and Jesus answered me, And I thought of you before I called you into being. "Jesus, in what way were You thinking about me?" In terms of admitting you to My eternal happiness. After these words, my soul was flooded with the love of God. I could not stop marveling at how much God loves us. (1292)

Transform me, Lord Jesus, ever present in the Eucharist; in my heart, my mind, and my soul; and in my life. Thank you for thinking about me before You called me into being. Help me think about You, and speak to You in my heart, many times every day. When I'm afraid — like the apostles and disciples were after You were placed in Your tomb — help me remember You never stop thinking about me, never stop loving me, never stop calling me home to You. Blessed be Your name forever.

The Adoration St. John Paul II Stations of the Cross

1. Jesus Prays in the Garden of Gethsemane
(Mt 26:36–41)

V. We adore You, O Christ, and we praise You.
R. Because by Your holy cross, You have redeemed the world.

During adoration, Jesus said to me, My daughter, know that your ardent love and the compassion you have for Me were a consolation to Me in the Garden [of Olives]. (1664)

Lord Jesus, let my love for You lead me to have more compassion for others. My Lord and my God, I adore You.

2. Jesus Is Betrayed by Judas and Arrested
(Mk 14:43–46)

V. *We adore You, O Christ, and we praise You.*
R. *Because by Your holy cross, You have redeemed the world.*

Jesus grew deeply troubled within
And said, "One of you will betray his Master."
They fell silent, with a silence as of the tomb…. (1002)

Time and again I have betrayed You, Lord Jesus. I have been silent as a tomb when You have called me to speak of the Way, the Truth, and the Life. Lord of Divine Mercy, help me be faithful. Help me be brave. My Lord and my God, I adore You.

3. Jesus Is Condemned by the Sanhedrin
(Lk 22:66–71)

V. *We adore You, O Christ, and we praise You.*
R. *Because by Your holy cross, You have redeemed the world.*

My daughter, when I was before Herod, I obtained a grace for you; namely, that you would be able to rise above human scorn and follow faithfully in My footsteps. (1164)

Lord Jesus, give me the grace to rise above human scorn and to follow Your footsteps more closely. My Lord and my God, I adore You.

4. Jesus Is Denied by Peter
(Mt 26:69–75)

V. *We adore You, O Christ, and we praise You.*
R. *Because by Your holy cross, You have redeemed the world.*

When one day I resolved to practice a certain virtue, I lapsed into the vice opposed to that virtue ten times more frequently than on other days. In the evening, I was reflecting on why, today, I had lapsed so extraordinarily, and I heard the words *[from Jesus]*: You were counting too much on yourself and too little on Me. And I understood the cause of my lapses. (1087)

Lord Jesus, help me remember that every time I fall, I deny You. And You are still there, with me. Lord Jesus, You know I love You. My Lord and my God, I adore You.

5. Jesus Is Judged by Pilate
(Mk 15:1–5, 15)

V. *We adore You, O Christ, and we praise You.*
R. *Because by Your holy cross, You have redeemed the world.*

[Jesus] would say, Consider My sufferings before Pilate. And thus, point by point, I meditated upon His sorrowful Passion for one week. (149)

Help me be with You, Lord Jesus, point by point, step by step, on your road to Calvary. On Your way to my redemption. My Lord and my God, I adore You.

6. Jesus Is Scourged at the Pillar and Crowned with Thorns
(Jn 19:1–3)

V. *We adore You, O Christ, and we praise You.*
R. *Because by Your holy cross, You have redeemed the world.*

… when I was making a Holy Hour, I saw how the Lord Jesus suffered as He was being scourged. Oh, such an inconceivable agony! How terribly Jesus suffered during the scourging! O poor sinners, on the day of judgment how will you face the Jesus whom you are now torturing so cruelly: His blood flowed to the ground, and in some places His flesh started to fall off. I saw a few bare bones on His back. The meek Jesus moaned softly and sighed. (188)

In the morning, during meditation, I felt a painful thorn in the left side of my head. The suffering continued all day. I meditated continually about how Jesus had been able to endure the pain of so many thorns which made up His crown. I joined my suffering to the sufferings of Jesus and offered it for sinners. (349)

Like St. Faustina, Lord Jesus, help me know Your presence when I suffer. Help me join my suffering to Yours for the good of others. My Lord and my God, I adore You.

7. Jesus Bears His Cross
(Jn 19:6, 15–17)

V. We adore You, O Christ, and we praise You.
R. Because by Your holy cross, You have redeemed the world.

O my Jesus, You alone know what persecutions I suffer…. You are my strength; sustain me that I may always carry out what You ask of me. Of myself I can do nothing, but when You sustain me, all difficulties are nothing for me. (91)

Lord Jesus, You did what the Father asked of You. Help me do what He asks of me. My Lord and my God, I adore You.

8. Jesus Is Helped by Simon of Cyrene to Carry His Cross
(Mk 15:21)

V. We adore You, O Christ, and we praise You.
R. Because by Your holy cross, You have redeemed the world.

Thank you, Jesus, for the graces and the pieces of the Cross which you give me at each moment of my life. (382)

I'm never alone, Lord Jesus. You are always there to help me carry my crosses. My Lord and my God, I adore You.

9. Jesus Meets the Women of Jerusalem
(Lk 23:27–31)

V. We adore You, O Christ, and we praise You.
R. Because by Your holy cross, You have redeemed the world.

All things will have an end in this vale of tears,
Tears will run dry and pain will cease.
Only one thing will remain —
Love for You, O Lord. (1132)

Lord Jesus, help me see You when others are in tears. Help me never lose sight of You when those tears are mine. My Lord and my God, I adore You.

10. Jesus Is Crucified
(Lk 23:33–34)

V. We adore You, O Christ, and we praise You.
R. Because by Your holy cross, You have redeemed the world.

I saw a great radiance and, in the midst of it, God the Father. Between this radiance and the earth I saw Jesus, nailed to the Cross in such a way that when God wanted to look at the earth, He had to look through the wounds of Jesus. And I understood that it was for the sake of Jesus that God blesses the earth. (60)

Lord Jesus, only begotten Son of the Father, for me and for my salvation You came down from heaven. For me, You were crucified, died, and were buried. My Lord and my God, I adore You.

11. Jesus Promises His Kingdom to the Good Thief
(Lk 23:39–43)

V. We adore You, O Christ, and we praise You.
R. Because by Your holy cross, You have redeemed the world.

O merciful Jesus, stretched on the cross, be mindful of the hour of our death. O most merciful Heart of Jesus, opened with a lance, shelter me at the last moment of my life. O Blood and Water, which gushed forth from the Heart of Jesus as a fount of unfathomable mercy for me at the hour of my death, O dying Jesus, Hostage of mercy, avert the Divine wrath at the hour of my death. (813)

Lord Jesus, remember me when the Father calls me home to Your kingdom. My Lord and my God, I adore You.

12. Jesus Speaks to His Mother and to the Beloved Disciple
(Jn 19:26–27)

V. We adore You, O Christ, and we praise You.
R. Because by Your holy cross, You have redeemed the world.

[The Mother of God said:] I am not only the Queen of Heaven, but also the Mother of Mercy and your Mother. (330)

Lord Jesus, thank you sharing Your clement, Your loving, Your sweet Blessed Mother with me. My Lord and my God, I adore You.

13. Jesus Dies on the Cross
(Lk 23:44–46)

V. *We adore You, O Christ, and we praise You.*
R. *Because by Your holy cross, You have redeemed the world.*

In the evening, I saw the Lord Jesus upon the cross. From His hands, feet, and side the Most Sacred Blood was flowing. After some time, Jesus said to me, All this is for the salvation of souls. Consider well, My daughter, what you are doing for their salvation. I answered, "Jesus, when I look at Your suffering, I see that I am doing next to nothing for the salvation of souls." And the Lord said to me, Know, My daughter, that your silent day-to-day martyrdom in complete submission to My will ushers many souls into heaven. And when it seems to you that your suffering exceeds your strength, contemplate My wounds, and you will rise above human scorn and judgment. Meditation on My passion will help you rise above all things. (1184)

Lord Jesus, into Your hands I give my life. My Lord and my God, I adore You.

14. Jesus Is Placed in the Tomb
(Mt 27:57–60)

V. *We adore You, O Christ, and we praise You.*
R. *Because by Your holy cross, You have redeemed the world.*

At the end of the hour, I went before the Blessed Sacrament and, like the greatest and most miserable of wretches, I begged for His mercy that He might heal and purify my poor soul. Then I heard these words, My daughter, all your miseries have been consumed in the flame of My love, like a little twig thrown into a roaring fire. By humbling yourself in this way, you draw upon yourself and upon other souls an entire sea of My mercy. I answered, "Jesus, mold my poor heart according to Your divine delight." (178)

Lord Jesus, mold my poor heart according to Your divine delight. My Lord and my God, I adore You.

15. Jesus Rises from the Dead
(Mt 28:1–10)

V. *We adore You, O Christ, and we praise You.*
R. *Because by Your holy cross, You have redeemed the world.*

Today, during the [Mass of the] Resurrection, I saw the Lord Jesus in the midst of a great light. He approached me and said, Peace be to you, My children, and He lifted up His hand and gave His blessing. The wounds in His hands, feet and side were indelible and shining. When he looked at me with such kindness and love, my whole soul drowned itself in Him. And he said to me, You have taken a great part in My Passion; therefore I now give you a great share in My joy and glory.... The kindness of Jesus is so great that I cannot express it. (205)

Lord Jesus, thank you for inviting me to take part in Your Passion and to share in Your joy and glory. My Lord and my God. All praise to You now and forever!

The Host of His Wounds

Then he said to Thomas, "Put your finger here, and see my hands;
and put out your hand, and place it in my side; do not be faithless,
but believing." Thomas answered him, "My Lord and my God!"
— JOHN 20:27–28

The Host that's adored in the monstrance, the Host that's received in Holy Communion, is the Body of a wounded Christ. A Christ marked and marred in His side, in each hand, in each foot. It was this Christ who told St. Faustina not to look away but to look more closely at His five wounds. To know that from them, "like from streams, mercy flows" (1190).

———

I dropped into the chapel for a moment, and then I heard this voice in my soul… the contemplation of My painful wounds is of great profit to you, and it brings Me great joy. (369)

I worshipped His five wounds, each one separately. (988)

By your wounds I have been healed.

May Your wounds be our shield against Your Father's justice. (611)

By your wounds I have been healed.

"Jesus, I love You more when I see You wounded and crushed with suffering like this than if I saw You in majesty." Jesus asked, Why? I replied, "Great majesty terrifies me, little nothing that I am and Your wounds draw me to Your Heart and tell me of your great love for me." After this conversation there was silence. I fixed my gaze upon His sacred wounds and felt happy to suffer with Him. I suffered, and yet I did not suffer, because I felt happy to know the depth of His love, and the hour passed like a minute. (252)

By your wounds I have been healed.

Jesus *[said:]* From all My wounds, like from streams, mercy flows for souls, but the wound in My Heart is the fountain of unfathomable mercy. From this fountain spring all graces for souls. (1190)

By your wounds I have been healed.

[Jesus said:] Remember My Passion, and if you do not believe My words, at least believe My wounds. (379)

[Jesus said:] And when it seems to you that your suffering exceeds your strength, contemplate My wounds, and you will rise above human scorn and judgment. Meditation on My passion will help you rise above all things. (1184)

By your wounds I have been healed.

And when this will of God will seem to me very harsh and difficult to fulfill, it is then I beg You, Jesus, may power and strength flow upon me from Your wounds, and may my lips keep repeating, "Your will be done, O Lord." (1265)

By your wounds I have been healed.

I must take refuge in the wounds of Jesus; I must seek consolation, comfort, light and affirmation in the wounds of Jesus. (226)

As I was praying before the Blessed Sacrament and greeting the five wounds of Jesus, at each salutation I felt a torrent of graces gushing into my soul, giving me a foretaste of heaven and absolute confidence in God's mercy. (1337)

Wounded Savior, Risen Christ, O Sacrament Most Holy, You bore my sins in Your body on the cross, so that, free from sins, I might live for righteousness. By your wounds I have been healed.

Hiding Oneself in the Five Sacred Wounds

Pious legend says Christ taught this prayer to St. Mechtilde (d. 1298) as she went to kiss the cross on Good Friday.

—

I thank you, O Lord Jesus Christ, for the painful wound of Your left foot, from which flowed the Precious Blood that washes away our sins. In it I sink and hide all the sins I have ever committed. Amen.

I thank you, O Lord Jesus Christ, for the painful wound of Your right foot, from which the fountain of peace flowed to us. In its depths I sink and bury all my desires that they may be purified and remain unspotted by any earthly stain. Amen.

I thank you, O Lord Jesus Christ, for the painful wound of Your left hand, from which the well of grace flowed to us. In it I enclose all my spiritual and bodily ills, that in union with Your sufferings they may become sweet to me, and by patience become a fragrant odor before God. Amen.

I thank you O Lord Jesus Christ, for the painful wound of Your right hand, from which the medicine of the soul was poured forth. In it I hide all my negli-

gences and omissions which I have committed in my virtuous exercises, that they may be atoned for by Your zealous works. Amen.

I thank you, O Lord Jesus Christ, for the healing wound of Your sweetest heart, from which living water and blood and the riches of all good flowed to us. I place myself in this wound, and there unite all my imperfect love to Your divine love, that thus it may be perfected. Amen.

The Precious Blood of Jesus

The Precious (and Powerful!) Blood of Jesus was a basic theme in St. Faustina's diary and in the prayer she composed that's now so widely used by others. That short, profound prayer is recited over and over — daily, globally — each time the Chaplet of Divine Mercy is said.

Describing its origin, St. Faustina wrote:

[Jesus to St. Faustina:] "... the contemplation of My painful wounds is of great profit to you and it brings me great joy" (369). St. Faustina fled to His wounds for healing and mercy.

The following day, Friday, September 13, 1935. In the evening, when I was in my cell [room] ... I saw the Most Holy Trinity. The greatness of Its majesty pierced me deeply.... At that very moment I felt in my soul the power of Jesus' grace, which dwells in my soul. When I became conscious of this grace, I was instantly snatched up before the Throne of God. Oh, how great is our Lord and God and how incomprehensible His holiness! I will make no attempt to describe this greatness, because before long we shall all see Him as He is. I found myself pleading with God for the world with words heard interiorly.... Never before had I prayed with such inner power as I did then. (474)

The words with which I entreated God are these: Eternal Father, I offer You the Body and Blood, Soul and Divinity of Your dearly beloved Son, Our Lord Jesus Christ, for our sins and those of the whole world; for the sake of His sorrowful Passion, have mercy on us. (475)

St. Faustina invites us — invites you — to offer your Eternal Father the blood of his dearly beloved Son. That very Precious Blood of Calvary and of the Eucharist. Offer the Eternal Father the Precious Blood of His Son for your loved ones, for the conversion of sinners, for the souls in Purgatory, for our Church, and for the sanctity of all members of the Body of Christ.

———

O Blood and Water, which gushed forth from the Heart of Jesus as a fount of mercy for us, I trust in You! (84)

Dear Jesus — who shed Your Most Precious Blood for me — I praise You, I thank You, I adore You.

O Jesus, be mindful of Your own bitter Passion and do not permit the loss of souls redeemed at so dear a price of Your most precious Blood. O Jesus, when I consider the great price of Your Blood, I rejoice at its immensity, for one drop alone would have been enough for the salvation of all sinners. (72)

Dear Jesus — who shed Your Most Precious Blood for me — I praise You, I thank You, I adore You.

During prayer I heard these words within me: The two rays *[of the Divine Mercy image]* denote Blood and Water. The pale ray stands for the Water which makes souls righteous. The red ray stands for the Blood which is the life of souls.... These two rays issued forth from the very depths of My tender mercy when My agonized Heart was opened by a lance on the Cross. (299)

Dear Jesus — who shed Your Most Precious Blood for me — I praise You, I thank You, I adore You.

[*Jesus said to St. Faustina:*] My Heart overflows with great mercy for souls, and especially for poor sinners. If only they could understand that I am the best of Fathers to them and that it is for them that the Blood and Water flowed from My Heart as from a fount overflowing with mercy. For them I dwell in the tabernacle as King of Mercy. (367)

Dear Jesus — who shed Your Most Precious Blood for me — I praise You, I thank You, I adore You.

[*St. Faustina said to Jesus:*] I sense keenly how Your Divine Blood is circulating in my heart; I have not the least doubt that Your most pure love has entered my heart with Your most sacred Blood. I am aware that You are dwelling in me, together with the Father and the Holy Spirit, or rather I am aware that it is I who am living in You, O incomprehensible God! I am aware that I am dissolving in You like a drop in an ocean. (478)

Dear Jesus — who shed Your Most Precious Blood for me — I praise You, I thank You, I adore You.

Jesus, You desired to dwell in my heart. Your living Blood unites with mine. Who can understand this close union? My heart encloses within itself the Almighty, the Infinite One. O Jesus, continue to grant me Your divine life. Let Your pure and noble Blood throb with all its might in my heart. I give You my whole being. Transform me into Yourself and make me capable of doing Your holy will in all things and of returning Your love. (832)

Dear Jesus — who shed Your Most Precious Blood for me — I praise You, I thank You, I adore You.

I am going forward through life amidst rainbows and storms, but with my head held high with pride, for I am a royal child. I feel that the blood of Jesus is circulating in my veins, and I have put my trust in the great mercy of the Lord. (992)

Dear Jesus — who shed Your Most Precious Blood for me — I praise You, I thank You, I adore You.

In the evening, I saw the Lord Jesus upon the cross. From His hands, feet, and side the Most Sacred Blood was flowing. After some time, Jesus said to me, All this is for the salvation of souls. (1184)

Dear Jesus — who shed Your Most Precious Blood for me — I praise You, I thank You, I adore You.

[Jesus said to St. Faustina:] Today bring to Me the souls who are in the prison of Purgatory, and immerse them in the abyss of My mercy. Let the torrents of My Blood cool down their scorching flames. All these souls are greatly loved by Me. They are making retribution to My justice. It is in your power to bring them relief. Draw all the indulgences from the treasury of My Church and offer them on their behalf. (1226)

Dear Jesus — who shed Your Most Precious Blood for me — I praise You, I thank You, I adore You.

[Jesus said to St. Faustina:] My Secretary, write that I am more generous toward sinners than toward the just. It was for their sake that I came down from heaven; it was for their sake that My Blood was spilled. Let them not fear to approach Me; they are most in need of My mercy. (1275)

Dear Jesus — who shed Your Most Precious Blood for me — I praise You, I thank You, I adore You.

[St. Faustina said to Jesus:] At the moment of Your death on the Cross, You bestowed upon us eternal life; allowing Your most holy side to be opened, You opened an inexhaustible spring of mercy for us, giving us Your dearest possession, the Blood and Water from Your Heart. Such is the omnipotence of Your mercy. From it all grace flows to us. (1747)

Dear Jesus — who shed Your Most Precious Blood for me — I praise You, I thank You, I adore You. "Transform me into Yourself and make me capable of doing Your holy will in all things and of returning Your love" (832). Amen.

V. Adoration in Times of Suffering

*Because he himself has suffered and been tempt-
ed, he is able to help those who are tempted.*
— HEBREWS 2:18

*He is able for all time to save those who draw near to God
through him, since he always lives to make intercession for them.*
— HEBREWS 7:25

Adoration During the "Dark Night of the Soul"

Like other saints and mystics, despite her faith, hard work, and perseverance, St. Faustina was no stranger to what's known as "the dark night of the
soul." No stranger to a feeling of the absence
of God rather than the overwhelming joy of
His presence. To the weight of daily community life and health problems crushing her
mentally, physically, and spiritually.

> [The convent's Mother Directress to St. Faus-tina:] "Have great con-fidence; God is always our Father, even when He sends us trials." (24)

Answering God's call, His invitation, to
sainthood can include times when there's
darkness, not light. Confusion, not clarity.
Despair, not hope. Still …

There is the call. There is the invitation.
There is the God who will never abandon you. Never forget you. Never stop
lavishing His infinite and eternal love on you.

I went before the Blessed Sacrament, and I began to speak to Jesus: "Jesus, You said that a mother would sooner forget her infant than God His creature, and that 'even if she would forget her infant, I, God, will never forget My creature.' O Jesus, do You hear how my soul is moaning? Deign to hear the painful whimpers of Your child. I trust in You, O God, because heaven and earth will pass, but Your word will last forever." Still, I found not a moment of relief. (23)

When my wordless prayers are moans and painful whimpers, hear me, Lord.

When my soul is in anguish, I think only in this way: Jesus is good and full of mercy, and even if the ground were to give way under my feet, I would not cease to trust in Him. (1192)

When my soul is in anguish, help me trust You even more, Lord.

O Jesus, today my soul is as though darkened by suffering. Not a single ray of light. The storm is raging, and Jesus is asleep. O my Master, I will not wake You; I will not interrupt Your sweet sleep. I believe that You fortify me without my knowing it.

Throughout the long hours I adore You, O living Bread, amidst the great drought in my soul. O Jesus, pure Love, I do not need consolations; I am nourished by Your will, O Mighty One! (195)

When my mind, my heart, my soul, and my life are raging, calm my stormy sea, Lord.

O my Jesus, despite the deep night that is all around me and the dark clouds which hide the horizon, I know that the sun never goes out. O Lord, though I cannot comprehend You and do not understand Your ways, I nonetheless trust in Your mercy. If it is Your will, Lord, that I live always in such darkness, may You be blessed. I ask You only one thing, Jesus: do not allow me to offend You in any way. O my Jesus, You alone know the longings and the sufferings of my heart. I am glad I can suffer for You, however little. When I feel that the suffering is more than I can bear, I take refuge in the Lord in the Blessed Sacrament, and I speak to Him with profound silence. (73)

When my nights are long and my days are dark, be the light of my world, Lord.

Once when I was being crushed by these dreadful sufferings, I went into the chapel and said from the bottom of my soul, "Do what You will with me, O Jesus, I will adore You in everything. May Your will be done in me, O my Lord and my God, and I will praise Your infinite mercy." Through this act of submission, these terrible torments left me. Suddenly I saw Jesus, who said to me, I am always in your heart. An inconceivable joy entered my soul, and a great love of God set my heart aflame. I see that God never tries us beyond what we are able to suffer. Oh, I fear nothing; if God sends such great suffering to a soul. He upholds it with an even greater grace, although we are not aware of it. One act of trust at such moments give greater glory to God than whole hours passed in prayer filled with consolations. (78)

When I am crushed by suffering, Lord, give me the faith to trust You, the hope to say "yes" to your will, and the love that is You.

Acts of Abandonment, Faith, Hope, Love, and Trust

In her Acts of Abandonment, Faith, Hope, Love, and Trust, St. Faustina shows us that despite her young age (she died at thirty-three) and very basic education (completing only three years of schooling), she was a mystic, theologian, and poet.

By her words — and much, much more so by her life — she shows us she was a saint.

Acts of Abandonment

Whatever You do with me, Jesus, I will always love You, for I am Yours. Little matter whether You leave me here or put me somewhere else; I am always Yours.

It is with love that I abandon myself to Your most wise decrees, O God, and Your will, O Lord, is my daily nourishment. (1145)

I abandon myself entirely to the action of Your grace. Let Your will be accomplished entirely in me, O Lord. (1326)

… the Mother of God gave me to experience the anxious concern she had in Her heart because of the Son of God. But this anxiety was permeated with such fragrance of abandonment to the will of God that I should call it rather a delight than an anxiety. (1437)

My Master, Guide Me

Jesus, source of life, sanctify me. O my strength, fortify me. My Commander, fight for me. Only light of my soul, enlighten me. My Master, guide me. I entrust myself to You as a little child does to its mother's love. Even if all things were to conspire against me, and even if the ground were to give way under my feet, I would be at peace close to Your Heart. You are always a most tender mother to me, and You surpass all mothers. I will sing of my pain to You by my silence, and You will understand me beyond any utterance. (1490)

Acts of Faith

Community life is difficult in itself, but it is doubly difficult to get along with proud souls. O God, give me a deeper faith that I may always see in every sister Your Holy Image which has been engraved in her soul. (1522)

I fervently beg the Lord to strengthen my faith, so that in my drab, everyday life I will not be guided by human dispositions, but by those of the spirit. Oh, how everything drags man towards the earth! But lively faith maintains the soul in the higher regions and assigns self-love its proper place; that is to say, the lowest one. (210)

I often ask the Lord Jesus for an intellect enlightened by faith. I express this to the Lord in these words: "Jesus, give me an intellect, a great intellect, for this only, that I may understand You better; because the better I get to know You, the more ardently will I love You. Jesus, I ask You for a powerful intellect, that I may understand divine and lofty matters. Jesus, give me a keen intellect with which I will get to know Your Divine Essence and Your indwelling, Triune life. Give my intellect these capacities and aptitudes by means of your special grace. Although I know that there is a capability through grace which the Church gives me, there is still a treasure of graces which You give us, O Lord, when we ask You for them. But if my request is not pleasing to You, then I beg You, do not give me the inclination to pray thus." (1474)

O Blessed Host: Faith

O Blessed Host, in golden chalice enclosed for me,
That through the vast wilderness of exile
I may pass — pure, immaculate, undefiled;
Oh, grant that through the power of Your love this might come to be.

O Blessed Host, take up Your dwelling within my soul,
O Thou my heart's purest love!
With Your brilliance the darkness dispel.
Refuse not Your grace to a humble heart.

O Blessed Host, enchantment of all heaven,
Though Your beauty be veiled
And captured in a crumb of bread,
Strong faith tears away that veil. (159)

Acts of Hope

My Jesus, my strength and my only hope, in You alone is all my hope.
(746)

… although it seems to me that You do not hear me, I put my trust
in the ocean of Your mercy, and I know that my hope will not be
deceived. (69)

O my God, my only hope, I have placed all my trust in You, and I
know I shall not be disappointed. (317)

O Blessed Host: Hope

O Blessed Host, our only hope in all the sufferings and adversities of life.

O Blessed Host, our only hope in the midst of darkness and of storms within and without.

O Blessed Host, our only hope in life and at the hour of our death.

O Blessed Host, our only hope in the midst of adversities and floods of despair.

O Blessed Host, our only hope in the midst of falsehood and treason.

O Blessed Host, our only hope in the midst of the darkness and god-lessness which inundate the earth.

O Blessed Host, our only hope in the longing and pain in which no one will understand us.

O Blessed Host, our only hope in the toil and monotony of everyday life.

O Blessed Host, our only hope amid the ruin of our hopes and endeavors.

O Blessed Host, our only hope in the midst of the ravages of the enemy and the efforts of hell. (356)

Acts of Love

My Jesus, You know that from my earliest years I have wanted to become a great saint; that is to say, I have wanted to love You with a love so great that there would be no soul who has hitherto loved You so. (1372)

O Christ, suffering for You is the delight of my heart and my soul. Prolong my sufferings to infinity, that I may give You a proof of my love. I accept everything that Your hand will hold out to me. Your love, Jesus, is enough for me. I will glorify You in abandonment and darkness, in agony and fear, in pain and bitterness, in anguish of spirit and grief of heart. In all things may You be blessed. My heart is so detached from the earth, that You Yourself are enough for me. There is no longer any moment in my life for self-concern. (1662)

O Jesus, keep me in holy fear, so that I may not waste graces. Help me to be faithful to the inspirations of the Holy Spirit. Grant that my heart may burst for love of You, rather than I should neglect even one act of love for You. (1557)

O My God

When I look into the future, I am frightened,
But why plunge into the future?
Only the present moment is precious to me,
As the future may never enter my soul at all.

It is no longer in my power,
To change, correct or add to the past;
For neither sages nor prophets could do that.
And so, what the past has embraced I must entrust to God.

O present moment, you belong to me, whole and entire,
I desire to use you as best I can.
And although I am weak and small,
You grant me the grace of Your omnipotence.

And so, trusting in Your mercy,
I walk through life like a little child,
Offering You each day this heart
Burning with love for Your greater glory. (2)

Acts of Trust

O Jesus, hidden in the Blessed Sacrament, ... With the trust and simplicity of a small child, I give myself to You today, O Lord Jesus, my Master. I leave You complete freedom in directing my soul. Guide me along the paths You wish. I won't question them. I will follow You trustingly. Your merciful Heart can do all things! (228)

O my God, my only hope, I have placed all my trust in You, and I know I shall not be disappointed. (317)

Trust, trust, O soul, though you are stained by sin,
For when you approach God, you will not taste bitterness.

Because He is a living fire of great love,
When we approach Him with sincerity,
Our miseries, sins and evil deeds vanish;
He will settle our debts when we surrender ourselves to Him. (1748)

O Blessed Host: Trust

O Blessed Host, I trust in You when the burdens are beyond my strength and I find my efforts are fruitless.

O Blessed Host, I trust in You when storms toss my heart about and my fearful spirit tends to despair.

O Blessed Host, I trust in You when my heart is about to tremble and mortal sweat moistens my brow.

O Blessed Host, I trust in You when everything conspires against me and black despair creeps into my soul.

O Blessed Host, I trust in You when my eyes will begin to grow dim to all temporal things and, for the first time, my spirit will behold the unknown worlds.

O Blessed Host, I trust in You when my tasks will be beyond my strength and adversity will become my daily lot.

O Blessed Host I trust in You when the practice of virtue will appear difficult for me and my nature will grow rebellious.

O Blessed Host, I trust in You when hostile blows will be aimed against me.

O Blessed Host, I trust in You when my toils and efforts will be misjudged by others.

O Blessed Host, I trust in You when Your judgments will resound over me; it is then that I will trust in the sea of Your mercy. (356)

Most Holy Trinity, I trust in Your infinite mercy. God is my Father and so I, His child, have every claim to His Divine Heart; and the greater the darkness, the more complete our trust should be. (357)

I do not understand how it is possible not to trust in Him who can do all things. With Him, everything; without Him, nothing. He is Lord. He will not allow those who have placed all their trust in Him to be put to shame. (358)

VI. St. Faustina's Prayers of Adoration

*I appeal to you therefore, brethren, by the mercies of
God, to present your bodies as a living sacrifice, holy and
acceptable to God, which is your spiritual worship.*
— ROMANS 12:1

Brief Moments and One-Minute Acts of Adoration

My happiest moments are when I am alone with my Lord. During these moments I experience the greatness of God. (289)

St. Faustina's close friend, Sister Crescentia, once said that when Sister Faustina was in front of the tabernacle she prayed fervently as she gazed radiantly at the altar. In her free moments at work, she frequently ran to the chapel to genuflect before Jesus in the Eucharist, whom she wanted to talk to whenever she could. (She encouraged the "wards" under her care to do the same.)

I entered the chapel for a moment and joy filled my soul. (216)

About midday, I entered the chapel for a moment, and again the power of grace struck my heart. (411)

I entered the chapel for a moment and heard a voice *[Jesus' voice]* in my soul saying, Why are you afraid? Do you think that I will not have enough omnipotence to support you? At that moment, my soul felt extraordinary strength, and all the adversities that could befall me in carrying out God's will seemed as nothing to me. (527)

When I entered the chapel for a moment that same evening, to thank God for all the graces He had bestowed on me in this house, suddenly God's presence enveloped me. (629)

"For a moment." For a minute. Or two. Eucharistic Adoration — and spiritual Eucharistic Adoration — have no requirement on how long they must last. It may last an hour, half an hour, fifteen, ten, or even five minutes.

Throughout the day it's possible to follow St. Faustina's example. Not necessarily rushing to the chapel but slowing down to spend a moment or two in simple adoration. Sometimes doing that before the tabernacle or the monstrance — and other times, wherever you may be.

If only for a moment, you can join St. Faustina in one of her small, tender prayers of adoration.

———

Adore, my soul, the mercy of the Lord. (1652)

Jesus, rest in my heart…. Jesus, hide me in Your Heart. (162)

My Jesus, penetrate me through and through so that I might be able to reflect You in my whole life…. I desire to reflect Your compassionate heart, full of mercy. (1242)

O Holy Trinity, make yourself known to souls! (592)

Praise and glory be to You, O Indivisible Trinity, One God, unto ages of ages! (278)

O my Lord, inflame my heart with love for You, that my spirit may not grow weary amidst the storms, the sufferings and the trials. You see how weak I am. Love can do all. (94)

O sweet, rose-red blood of Jesus, ennoble my blood and change it into Your own blood, and let this be done to me according to Your good pleasure. (1575)

My only hope is in You. (76)

I hope against all hope in the ocean of Your mercy. (309)

I adore You, O living Bread. (195)

Hail, living Host! (162)

Jesus, I love You with all my heart! (239)

O my Jesus, I thank You for Your Heart — it is all I need. (240)

I also beg you, Jesus, to free all souls from purgatory. (240)

O my Jesus, save me. (1558)

O Jesus, concealed in the Blessed Sacrament of the Altar, my only love and mercy, I commend to You all the needs of my body and soul. You can help me, because You are Mercy itself. In You lies all my hope. (1751)

O Jesus, my strength, You alone can help me; grant me fortitude. (1066)

O Divine Will, be my love! (725)

O sweet little Jesus, here is my heart; let it be a little cozy dwelling place for Yourself. (845)

Today, Jesus, I offer You all my sufferings, mortifications and prayers. (341)

Jesus, I trust in You! (239)

> ## JESUS, FRIEND OF A LONELY HEART
>
> "Jesus, Friend of a lonely heart, You are my heaven. You are my peace. You are my salvation, You are my serenity in moments of struggle and amidst an ocean of doubts. You are the bright ray that lights up the path of my life. You are everything to a lonely soul. You understand the soul even though it remains silent. You know our weaknesses, and like a good physician, You comfort and heal, sparing us sufferings — expert that You are." (247)

A Living Host

When St. Faustina wrote about the "host," she meant it in two distinct, but overlapping, ways. The first — with a capital *H* — was Our Lord in the Eucharist. The second — with a lowercase *h* — was herself.

Over and over throughout the diary, the young nun used the image of a host to describe what she wanted to do, what she wanted to become, despite being confined to a convent. And what was St. Faustina's goal? In her own small ways, and through her own painful and personal experiences, it was to imitate the suffering and sacrifice of Christ and join her suffering and sacrifice to His. All that and, at the same time, to praise her Savior and silently endure all hardships for the salvation of souls.

Like Jesus in the Host, she wanted to be "hidden" in hers. She wanted to be a "little wafer wherein the eye perceives nothing, and yet … a host consecrated" to Christ (641).

———

When I had received Jesus in Holy Communion, my heart cried out with all its might, "Jesus, transform me into another host! I want to be a living host for You. You are a great and all-powerful Lord; You can grant me this favor." And the Lord answered me, You are a living host, pleasing to the Heavenly Father. But reflect: What is a host? A sacrifice. And so...?

O my Jesus, I understand the meaning of "host," the meaning of sacrifice. I desire to be before Your Majesty a living host; that is, a living sacrifice that daily burns in Your honor....

O living Host, light of my soul! (1826)

Dear Faustina, pray for me and for my loved ones.

When I came to the adoration ... [a] vision passed before the eyes of my soul; it was like the vision Jesus had in the Garden of Olives. First, the physical sufferings and all the circumstances that would increase them; [then] the full scope of the spiritual sufferings and those that no one would know about. Everything entered into the vision: false suspicions, loss of good name.... [W]hat I went through later on was in no way different from what I had known at that moment. My name is to be: "sacrifice." (135)

Dear Faustina, pray for me and for my loved ones.

My name is host — or sacrifice, not in words but in deeds, in the emptying of myself and in becoming like You on the Cross, O Good Jesus, my Master! (485)

Dear Faustina, pray for me and for my loved ones.

Jesus, hide me; just as You have hidden Yourself under the form of the white Host, so hide me from human eyes, and particularly hide the gifts which You so kindly grant me. May I not betray outwardly what You are affecting in my soul. I am a white host before you, O Divine Priest. Consecrate me Yourself, and may my transubstantiation be known only to You. I stand before You each day as a sacrificial host and implore Your mercy upon the world. In silence, and unseen. I will empty myself before You; my pure and undivided love will burn, in profound silence, as a holocaust. (1564)

Dear Faustina, pray for me and for my loved ones.

My heart is a living tabernacle in which the living Host is reserved. I have never sought God in some far-off place, but within myself. It is in the depths of my own being that I commune with my God. (1302)

Dear Faustina, pray for me and for my loved ones.

On the First Friday of the month, before Communion, I saw a large ciborium filled with sacred hosts. A hand placed the ciborium in front of me, and I took it in my hands. There were a thousand living hosts inside. Then I heard a voice *[from Jesus]*, These are hosts which have been received by the souls for whom you have obtained the grace of true conversion during this Lent. That was a week before Good Friday. I spent the day in great interior recollection, emptying myself for the sake of souls. (640)

Dear Faustina, pray for me and for my loved ones.

Oh, what joy it is to empty myself for the sake of immortal souls! I know that the grain of wheat must be destroyed and ground between millstones in order to become food. In the same way, I must become destroyed in order to be useful to the Church and souls, even though exteriorly no one will notice my sacrifice. O Jesus, outwardly I want to be hidden, just like this little wafer wherein the eye perceives nothing, and yet I am a host consecrated to You. (641)

Dear Faustina, pray for me and for my loved ones. Amen.

I Am a Host in Your Hand, O Jesus

I am a host in Your hand,
O Jesus, my Creator and Lord,
Silent, hidden, without beauty or charm,
Because all the beauty of my soul is imprinted within me.

I am a host in Your hand, O Divine Priest,
Do with me as You please;
I am totally dependent on Your will, O Lord
Because it is the delight and adornment of my soul.

I am like a white host in Your hand, O God,
I implore You, transform me into Yourself.
May I be wholly hidden in You,
Locked in Your merciful Heart as in Heaven.

I am like a host in Your hand, O Eternal Priest,
May the wafer of my body hide me from human eye;
May Your eye alone measure my love and devotion,
Because my heart is always united with Your Divine Heart.

I am like a sacrificial host in Your hand, O Divine Mediator,
And I burn on the altar of holocaust,
Crushed and ground by suffering like grains of wheat,
And all this for the sake of Your glory, for the salvation of souls.

I am a host abiding in the tabernacle of Your Heart.
I go through life drowned in Your love,
And I fear nothing in the world,
For You Yourself are my shield, my strength, and my defense.

I am a host, laid on the altar of Your Heart,
To burn forever with the fire of love,
For I know that You have lifted me up solely because of Your mercy,
And so I turn all the gifts and graces to Your glory.

I am a host in Your hand, O Judge and Savior.
In the last hour of my life,
May the omnipotence of Your grace lead me to my goal,
May Your compassion on the vessel of mercy become famous. (1629)

St. Faustina's Litany to the Living Host

Jesus, living Host, ... You are my all! It is with simplicity and love, with faith and trust that I will always come to You, O Jesus! I will share everything with You, as a child with its loving mother, my joys and sorrows — in a word, everything. (230)

Lord, have mercy!

O Sacred Host, fountain of divine sweetness,
You give strength to my soul;
O You are the Omnipotent One, who took flesh of the Virgin,
You come to my heart, in secret,
Beyond reach of the groping senses. (1233)

Christ, have mercy!

O white Host, You preserve my soul in whiteness; I fear the day when I might forsake You. You are the Bread of Angels, and thus also the Bread of Virgins. (1350)

Lord, have mercy!

Let us pray:

O living Host, my one and only strength, fountain of love and mercy, embrace the whole world, fortify faint souls. Oh, blessed be the instant and the moment when Jesus left us His most merciful Heart! (223)

Amen. Alleluia!

St. Faustina's Poetic Praise and Hymns

St. Faustina's spirituality was also reflected in poetic praise and hymns. She loved to sing. She sang until her illness made it impossible. Her two favorite hymns were "I Must Honor Jesus Hidden in the Eucharist" and "Good Night, O Holy Head of My Jesus." They prompted her to express her own feeling for Him.

Faustina was enchanted with creation until the end. She wrote this reflection in honor God's infinite goodness and the beauty of all His creation.

Adoration of the Creator

Be adored, O our Creator and Lord.
O universe, humbly glorify your God;
Thank your Creator to the best of your powers
And praise God's incomprehensible mercy.

Come, O earth, in all your fine greenery;
Come, you too, O fathomless sea.

Let your gratitude become a loving song
And sing the greatness of God's mercy.

Come, beautiful, radiant sun.
Come, bright dawn which precedes it.
Join in one hymn, and let your clear voices
Sing in one accord God's great mercy.

Come, hills and valleys, sighing woods and thickets,
Come, lovely flowers of morningtide;
Let your unique scent
Adore and glorify God's mercy.

Come, all you lovely things of earth,
Which man does not cease to wonder at.
Come, adore God in your harmony,
Glorifying God's inconceivable mercy.

Come, indelible beauty of all the earth,
And, with great humility, adore your Creator,
For all things are locked in His mercy,
With one mighty voice all things cry out; how great is the mercy
    of God.

But above all these beauties,
A more pleasing praise to God
Is a soul innocent and filled with childlike trust,
Which, through grace, is closely bound to Him. (1750)

O Jesus, concealed in the Blessed Sacrament of the Altar, my only love
and mercy, I commend to You all the needs of my body and soul. You can
help me, because You are Mercy itself. In You lies all my hope. (1751)

I Must Honor Jesus Hidden in the Eucharist

Jesus hidden in the Sacrament I am to adore,
Give up all for Him, and live by His love.
He gives Himself to us, with us He took up His abode;
For His divine glory, let us consecrate our life to Him.
With faith I must humble the senses and my mind,
For there is no longer bread here, it's God, it is my Jesus.

Here, Hosanna, continuously sings the Angelic choir to Him,
And this never-ending worship is for us, poor ones, an example.
To share exile with us is His delight:
O that abiding with Him may always be my joy!
He knows what anguish is, He's acquainted with tears of sadness;
I will tell Him my suffering, for my heart trembles with pain.

My Sweetest Jesus, O heaven of my soul,
You are a blissful Spring amidst the earthly drought.
In the Cenacle to Your disciples You gave Yourself but once;
To us on the altar, as in heaven, You became [our] daily bread.
I would like to be an Angel, who continually sings Your glory,
Offering my heart to You with face all aglow.

Grant that this lamp of mine brightly shine Your light,
Until death with its cold breath extinguishes its flame.
Let the song of Your love ring out till my dying day.
Here at foot of Your throne, I swear to You my fidelity.
Concerned always for Your honor I want to go there,
Where among the heaven's glory, You're alone the happiness of all.

(The composer of the hymn above is not known. It is very popular and is used at Eucharistic feasts, especially First Holy Communion celebrations, worldwide.)

Good Night, O Holy Head of My Jesus

Good night, Holy Head of My Jesus,
who was wounded in body and mind.
Good night, rosy flower,
Good night, beloved Jesus, goodnight!
Good night, holy hair, heavily torn,
and stained with most sacred Blood.
Good night ...
Good night, holy neck, chained and shackled,
Be praised for all eternity.
Good night ...
Good night, holy hands, outstretched on the Cross,
As the strings of the lute, when they are turned.
Good night ...
Good night, holy side, from which flowed
Holy Blood and washed the sins of man.
Good night ...

VII. The Graces of Silent Adoration Without Words

"Be still, and know that I am God."
— PSALM 46:10

Silent Adoration

Deep love doesn't always need words. At times, they get in the way. It's the presence, the being there together, the being with each other, that says what words are incapable of saying.

Just as a longtime, happily-married couple or two good friends can go out to dinner and have a lovely evening with neither speaking very much, so too with St. Faustina before the Blessed Sacrament.

The value and blessing of silence is a common theme in her diary. It was a lesson she continued to learn as she strove to become better at it. To be still. To listen. To just be with.

And what she came to understand about silence before the Blessed Sacrament, she applied in her daily life among the other members of her religious community. At times, she made a deliberate effort to keep silent.

All that can be true in your life too. With patience, with practice, you can come to say less, whether aloud or mentally, as you move closer to Christ and better realize how close He is to you — how close to you He wants to be!

And outside those chapel walls, you can begin to better recognize and appreciate the wisdom and comfort that silence can bring. To notice the impact that your speaking even a little less and listening even a little more can have on those around you.

Describing silence within the chapel, St. Faustina wrote:

Silence is so powerful a language that it reaches to the throne of the living God. Silence is His language, though secret, yet living and powerful. (888)

Patience, prayer and silence — these are what give strength to the soul. (944)

My particular examen is still the same; namely, union with the merciful Christ, and silence. The flower which I lay at the feet of the Mother of God for May is my practice of silence. (1105)

The Lord gave me to know how displeased He is with a talkative soul. *[He said:]* I find no rest in such a soul. The constant din tires Me, and in the midst of it the soul cannot discern My voice. (1008)

A silent soul is strong; no adversities will harm it if it perseveres in silence. The silent soul is capable of attaining the closest union with God. It lives almost always under the inspiration of the Holy Spirit. God works in a silent soul without hindrance. (477)

But, in order to hear the voice of God, one has to have silence in one's soul and to keep silence; not a gloomy silence, but an interior silence; that is to say, recollection in God. (118)

Advent is approaching. I want to prepare my heart for the coming of the Lord Jesus by silence and recollection of spirit, uniting myself with the Most Holy Mother and faithfully imitating Her virtue of silence, by which She found pleasure in the eyes of God Himself. I trust that, by Her side, I will persevere in this resolution. (1398)

And when considering the virtue of speaking less frequently outside the chapel, St. Faustina said, prayed ... and admitted:

O Blessed Host, support me and seal my lips against all murmuring and complaint. When I am silent, I know I shall be victorious. (896)

Silence is a sword in the spiritual struggle. A talkative soul will never attain sanctity. The sword of silence will cut off everything that would like to cling to the soul. We are sensitive to words and quickly want to answer back, without taking any regard as to whether it is God's will that we should speak. (477)

Whenever I receive Holy Communion, I will ask Jesus to fortify and cleanse my tongue that I may not injure my neighbor with it. (375)

When I receive Jesus in Holy Communion, I ask Him fervently to deign to heal my tongue so that I would offend neither God nor neighbor by it. I want my tongue to praise God without cease. Great are the faults committed by the tongue. The soul will not attain sanctity if it does not keep watch over its tongue. (92)

I sometimes talk too much. A thing could be settled in one or two words, and as for me, I take too much time about it. But Jesus wants me to use that time to say some short-indulgenced prayers for the souls in purgatory. And the Lord says that every word will be weighed on the day of judgment. (274)

THE PERFECT SILENCE OF GOD

- "There is nothing littler, meeker, or more silent than Christ present in the Host. This little piece of bread embodies the humility and perfect silence of God, his tenderness, and his love for us."

- "The desire to see God is what urges us to love solitude and silence. For silence is where God dwells. He drapes himself in silence."

- "In the silence of the heart God speaks. If you face God in prayer and silence, God will speak to you. Then you will know that you are nothing. It is only when you realize your nothingness, your emptiness, that God can fill you with himself. Souls of prayer are souls of great silence."

- "Because true Christian silence is a welcoming space, an adoring pause in our endless interior monologues, carved out in order to receive the One who created us in silence and calls us back into stillness to meet him there."

- "While God will — and does — meet us anywhere, he doesn't like to shout. He prefers whispers to earthquakes, shattering winds, roaring fires (1 Kings 19:11–13). When we wonder where he is, we may have to creatively seek out a little stillness; an adoration chapel for holy silence filled with God."

— Cardinal Robert Sarah, *The Power of Silence*

The Adoration Litany of Silence

Dearest Lord, as I come into Your presence in the Most Blessed Sacrament, help me trust in the silence we can share as You:

Ease my mind.
Word-made-flesh who needs no words, I adore You.

Calm my heart.
Word-made-flesh who needs no words, I adore You.

Soothe my spirit.
Word-made-flesh who needs no words, I adore You.

Fill my soul.
Word-made-flesh who needs no words, I adore You.

Dearest Lord, as I come into your presence in those I meet during my day, help me quietly:

Ease their minds.
Word-made-flesh who needs no words, I adore You.

Calm their hearts.
Word-made-flesh who needs no words, I adore You.

Soothe their spirits.
Word-made-flesh who needs no words, I adore You.

Help them be open to the graces with which you wish to fill their souls.
Word-made-flesh who needs no words, I adore You.

Dearest Lord, help me be silent and know that You are God. Amen.

VIII. Four Sisters — Four Saints — on Adoration of the Sacred Heart

One of the soldiers pierced his side with a spear,
and at once there came out blood and water.
— JOHN 19:34

Two women religious remained tucked away in convents and were assigned basic tasks in their community.

Two others traveled the world and were well known for the work they did in service to the poor, the sick, and the dying.

The two nuns who lived in relative obscurity were mystics and visionaries. Sister Margaret Mary established the Devotion to the Sacred Heart (the First Fridays and Holy Hours), and Sister Faustina introduced Jesus as Divine Mercy (now marked annually on the Sunday after Easter, and daily with the Divine Mercy Chaplet).

The two globetrotters — Mother Cabrini and Mother Teresa — were movers and shakers, each founding a thriving religious order to expand and carry on her work, her mission.

None had an easy life. None hesitated to make personal sacrifices and accept personal crosses.

Each relied heavily on Eucharistic Adoration and had a deep devotion to the Sacred Heart. Each wanted others — indeed, wanted everyone — to know what a blessing, a grace, a truly divine gift Eucharistic Adoration is.

Sister Margaret Mary Alacoque

Order of the Visitation of Holy Mary
1647–1690

"O Mary, Mother of Jesus Christ, and our dear Mother! O all you holy angels, who, by your adoration in our churches, make up for the little love which your God and our Savior receives from men, obtain for us the grace to comprehend a little of the love of Jesus Christ in the Most Holy Sacrament."

[Jesus said to Sister Margaret Mary:] "I have a burning thirst to be honored by men in the Blessed Sacrament, and I find hardly anyone who strives, according to My desire, to allay this thirst by making Me some return of love."

"I desire but this one grace, and long to be consumed like a burning candle in His holy Presence every moment of the life that remains to me. For that I would be willing, I think, to suffer all the pains imaginable till judgment day, if only I should not have to leave His sacred presence. My only motive would be to be consumed in honoring Him and to acknowledge that burning love He shows us in this wonderful Sacrament. Here His love holds Him captive till the end of time. It is of this one can truly say, 'Love triumphs, love enjoys, Love finds in God its joys.' "

Praying with St. Margaret Mary

"From the depth of my nothingness, I prostrate myself before You, O Most Sacred, Divine and Adorable Heart of Jesus, to pay You all the homage of love, praise and adoration in my power. Amen."

"Take away, O my Jesus, the blindness of my heart, that I may know You.

"Take away the coldness of my heart, that I may resist everything that is contrary to Your will.

"Take away its heavy earthly sluggishness and selfishness, that I may be capable of heroic sacrifice for Your glory, and for the souls whom You have redeemed with Your own most Precious Blood. Amen."

Sister Maria Faustina Kowalska

Sisters of Our Lady of Mercy
1905–1938

Praying with St. Faustina

I adore You, O living Bread, amidst the great drought in my soul. (195)

O great, incomprehensible God,
Who had deigned to abase Yourself so,
Humbly I adore you
And beg You in Your goodness to save me. (1231)

I adore You, Lord and Creator, hidden in the Blessed Sacrament. I adore You for all the works of Your hands, that reveal to me so much wisdom, goodness and mercy, O Lord. You have spread so much beauty over the earth, and it tells me about Your beauty, even though these beautiful things are but a faint reflection of You, Incomprehensible Beauty.... And, although my worship is so little and poor,

I am at peace because I know that You know it is sincere, however inadequate. (1692)

May You be adored, O merciful God of ours,
O All-powerful Lord and Creator.
In deepest humility, we give You praise,
Plunging ourselves into the ocean of your Godhead. (1744)

Be adored, O God, in the work of Your mercy,
Be blessed by all faithful hearts
On whom Your gaze rests
In whom dwells Your immortal life. (1748)

Mother Frances Xavier Cabrini

Missionary Sisters of the Sacred Heart of Jesus (Founder)
1850–1917

"Go often, my dear ones, and place yourself at the feet of Jesus. He is our comfort, our way, and our life."

"Remember that the Blessed Sacrament is like a pillar of fire that is our light and guide."

Praying with St. Frances Xavier Cabrini

"Almighty God, kneeling before Your Divine Majesty, I adore You and because You command me, I dare approach Your divine Heart. But what shall I say if You do not enlighten me with a ray of Your divine light?

"Speak to my soul, O Lord, and command me to listen to Your voice. Enlighten my will to put Your words into practice. Pour Your grace into my heart; lift up my soul weighed down by my sins; raise my mind to heavenly things, so that earthly desires may no longer appeal to me.

"Speak to my soul with Your divine omnipotence, for You are my salvation, my life, and my peace, in time and in eternity."

Litany of the Sacred Heart of Jesus
(By St. Frances Xavier Cabrini)

Loving Heart of Jesus,	attract me!
All powerful Heart of Jesus,	win me to Yourself!
Unchanging Heart of Jesus,	keep me constant!
Immensity of the Heart of Jesus,	fill me!
Holiness of the Heart of Jesus,	make me holy!
Providence of the Heart of Jesus,	assist me!
Obedience of the Heart of Jesus,	make me docile!
Silence of the Heart of Jesus,	teach me!
Purity of the Heart of Jesus,	purify me!
Patience of the Heart of Jesus,	bear with me!
Desires of the Heart of Jesus,	rule in me!
Flames of the Heart of Jesus,	set me on fire!
Kindness of the Heart of Jesus,	encircle me!
Sufferings of the Heart of Jesus,	make me compassionate!
Riches of the Heart of Jesus,	satisfy me!
Humiliations of the Heart of Jesus,	overwhelm me!
Graces of the Heart of Jesus,	flood me!
Sacred Heart of Jesus, my King,	possess me!

Sacred Heart, my Father,	give me life!
Sacred Heart, my Teacher,	instruct me!
Sacred Heart, my Guide,	lead me!
Sacred Heart, Physician,	heal me!
Sacred Heart, my Judge,	pardon me!
Sacred Heart, my Savior,	save me!
Sacred Heart, my God,	be my All!
Sacred Heart, my All,	MAKE ME ALL YOURS!

Mother Teresa of Calcutta

Missionaries of Charity (Founder)
1910–1997

"When the Sisters are exhausted, up to their eyes in work; when all seems to go awry, they spend an hour in prayer before the Blessed Sacrament. This practice has never failed to bear fruit: they experience peace and strength."

"The Eucharist is connected with the Passion. If Jesus had not established the Eucharist we would have forgotten the Crucifixion. It would have faded into the past and we would have forgotten that Jesus loved us. There is a saying that to be far away from the eyes is to be far away from the heart. To make sure that we do not forget, Jesus gave us the Eucharist as a memorial of His love…. When you look at the Crucifix, you understand how much Jesus loved you then, when you look at the Sacred Host you understand how much Jesus loves you now."

"Jesus has made Himself the Bread of Life to give us life. Night and day, He is there. If you really want to grow in love, come back to the Eucharist, come back to that Adoration."

"A Holy Hour of adoration helps bring everlasting peace to your soul and in your family. It brings us personal peace and strength. It brings us a greater love for Jesus, for each other, and for the poor. Every holy hour deepens our union with Him and bears much fruit."

Praying with St. Teresa of Calcutta

"Oh Jesus, You who suffer, grant that today and every day I may be able to see You in the person of Your sick ones, and that by offering them my care, I may serve You. Grant that, even if You are hidden under the unattractive disguise of anger, of crime, or of mental illness, I may recognize You and say, 'Jesus, You who suffer, how sweet it is to serve You.' … Lord, increase my faith. Bless my efforts and my work, now and forever. Amen."

CONSECRATION TO THE SACRED HEART OF JESUS

Adorable Heart of Jesus, the tenderest, the most amiable, the most generous of all hearts, penetrated with gratitude at the sight of Your benefits, I come to consecrate myself wholly and unreservedly to You! I wish to devote all my energies to promoting Your worship and winning, if possible, all hearts to You. Receive my heart this day, O Jesus. Amen.

IX. Private Adoration After Receiving Holy Communion

"If a man loves me, he will keep my word, and my Father will love him, and we will come to him and make our home with him."
— JOHN 14:23

Throughout her diary, St. Faustina shares what she prayed, thought, felt, and experienced during her time of "private adoration" after receiving Our Lord in the Blessed Sacrament.

Even for the rest of us — for the vast majority of us — who will never be mystics or visionaries, Christ is present in us in a particular way after receiving Holy Communion. And for all of us, it can be a time of private one-on-one adoration with the One who created us.

The One who created you.

Yes, St. Faustina was "greatly favored," but that doesn't mean she was more loved — more cherished — than you are. God loves you, just as He loves the Blessed Mother, just as He loves St. Faustina ... infinitely.

And personally.

What He says to you won't be identical in all ways to what He said to them. And what you say to Him, with words or in your heart, won't perfectly match what they said to Him. The relationship you and God share is unique. One of a kind. Forever.

But like St. Faustina, "after Holy Communion" you have the opportunity to adore that personal, all-loving God — your God — as His beloved son or daughter.

———

After Holy Communion, when I had welcomed Jesus into my heart, I said to Him, "My Love, reign in the most secret recesses of my heart, there where my most secret thoughts are conceived, where You alone have free access, in this deepest sanctuary where human thought cannot penetrate. May You alone dwell there, and may everything I do exteriorly take its origin in You. I ardently desire, and I am striving with all the strength of my soul, to make You, Lord, feel at home in this sanctuary." (1721)

I often feel God's presence after Holy Communion in a special and tangible way. I know God is in my heart…. I live in Him and He in me. I am never alone, because He is my constant companion. He is present to me at every moment. Our intimacy is very close, through a union of blood and of life. (318)

After Holy Communion, I felt the beating of the Heart of Jesus in my own heart. Although I have been aware, for a long time, that Holy Communion continues in me until the next Communion, today — and throughout the whole day — I am adoring Jesus in my heart and asking Him, by His grace, to protect little children from the evil that threatens them. A vivid and even physically felt presence of God continues throughout the day and does not in the least interfere with my duties. (1821)

Today, I only received Holy Communion and stayed for a few moments of the Mass. All my strength is in You, O Living Bread. It would be difficult for me to live through the day if I did not receive Holy Communion. It is my shield; without You, Jesus, I know not how to live. (814)

Once after Holy Communion, I heard these words: You are Our dwelling place. At that moment, I felt in my soul the presence of the Holy Trinity, the Father, the Son, and the Holy Spirit. I felt that I was the temple of God. I felt I was a child of the Father. I cannot explain all this, but the spirit understands it well. O Infinite Goodness, how low You stoop to Your miserable creature! (451)

Jesus, when You come to me in Holy Communion, You who, together with the Father and the Holy Spirit, have deigned to dwell in the little heaven of my heart, I try to keep You company throughout the day, I do not leave You alone for even a moment.... I then try to make it easier for Jesus to pass through me to other souls. I go everywhere with Jesus; His presence accompanies me everywhere. (486)

After Holy Communion: I saw Jesus in the usual way, and He spoke these words to me: Lay your head on My shoulder, rest and regain your strength. I am always with you. (498)

After Holy Communion, I saw the Lord Jesus, who said these words to me: Today, penetrate into the spirit of My poverty and arrange everything in such a way that the most destitute will have no reason to envy you. I find pleasure, not in large buildings and magnificent structures, but in a pure and humble heart. (532)

After Holy Communion, I suddenly saw the Lord Jesus, who spoke these words to me: Now I know that it is not for the graces or gifts that you love me, but because My will is dearer to you than life. (707)

"I HAVE ONLY ONE TASK"

On a one-day retreat on January 30, 1938, less than nine months before she passed away, St. Faustina wrote:

> In the meditation on death, I asked the Lord to deign to fill my heart with those sentiments which I will have at the moment of my death. And through God's grace I received an interior reply that I had done what was within my power and so could be at peace. At that moment, such profound gratitude to God was awakened in my soul that I burst into tears of joy like a little child. I prepared to receive Holy Communion next morning as "viaticum" [one's final Communion before death], and I said the prayers of the dying for my own intention. (1551)
>
> O my Jesus, I have only one task to carry out in my lifetime, in death, and throughout eternity, and that is to adore Your incomprehensible mercy. (1553)

In the morning, after Holy Communion, my soul was immersed in the Godhead. I was united to the Three Divine Persons in such a way that when I was united to Jesus, I was simultaneously united to the Father and to the Holy Spirit, My soul was flooded with joy beyond understanding, and the Lord gave me to experience the whole ocean and abyss of His fathomless mercy. (1073)

On Friday, after Holy Communion, I was carried in spirit before the throne of God. There I saw the heavenly Powers which incessantly praise God. Beyond the throne I saw a brightness inaccessible to creatures, and there only the Incarnate Word enters as Mediator. When

Jesus entered this light, I heard these words, Write down at once what you hear: ... If I call creatures into being — that is the abyss of My mercy. (85)

Thank You, O Jesus, for Holy Communion
In which You give us Yourself.
I feel Your Heart beating within my breast
As You cause Your divine life to unfold within me. (1286)

X. Adoration with the Angels

Bless the LORD, O you his angels,
you mighty ones who do his word,
hearkening to the voice of his word!
Bless the LORD, all his hosts,
his ministers that do his will!
— PSALM 103:20–21

The Blessed Sacrament is fittingly called the "Bread of Angels" because of the ardent love with which the angels cherish the Sacred Host and the profound adoration which they render to the hidden God.

Unite your intention with that of your guardian angel to adore the Blessed Sacrament. Our angel helps us to personal union with God, who wishes to enter our hearts. How willing our angel is to pray with us, to strengthen us in our prayers and sacrifices. They join invisibly with us in adoration.

St. Faustina reveals in her diary that she had a very close relationship with her guardian angel, praying to him daily. She had no doubt that he protected her with his presence and helped her in ordinary life.

She also writes how he showed her purgatory, asked her to pray for the dying, and assisted her in spiritual battles.

No wonder she took delight in joining her prayers with the angels, asking them to help her give praise and glory to God!

O King of Glory, though you hide your beauty, yet the eye of my soul rends the veil. I see the angelic choirs giving You honor without cease…. (80)

I immediately asked my Guardian Angel for help, and at once the bright and radiant figure of my Guardian Angel appeared.... His look was modest and peaceful, and a flame of fire sparked from his forehead. (419)

Jesus, delight of my soul, Bread of Angels,
My whole being is plunged in You,
And I live Your divine life as do the elect in heaven,
And the reality of this life will not cease, though I be laid in the
    grave. (1393)

Then I saw one of the seven spirits near me, radiant as at other times, under a form of light. I constantly saw him beside me when I was riding on the train. I saw an angel standing on every church we passed, but surrounded by a light which was paler than that of the spirit who was accompanying me on the journey, and each of these spirits who were guarding the churches bowed his head to the spirit who was near me.

When I entered the convent gate at Warsaw, the spirit disappeared. I thanked God for His goodness, that He gives us angels for companions. Oh, how little people reflect on the fact that they always have beside them such a guest, and at the same time a witness to everything! Remember, sinners, that you likewise have a witness to all your deeds. (630)

Although You take the form of a little Child, I see in You the immortal, infinite Lord of lords, whom pure spirits adore, day and night, and for whom the hearts of the Seraphim burn with the fire of purest love. O Christ, O Jesus, I want to surpass them in my love for You! I apologize to you, O pure spirits, for my boldness in comparing myself to you. I, this chasm of misery, this abyss of misery; and You, O God, who are the incomprehensible abyss of mercy, swallow me up as the heat of the sun swallows up a drop of dew! A loving look from You will fill up any abyss. I feel immensely happy at the greatness of God. Seeing God's greatness is more than enough to make me happy throughout all eternity! (334)

Prayers to the Angels

All the houses in St. Faustina's congregation had statues of St. Michael the Archangel, the "Guardian of the Blessed Sacrament." Tradition holds that his work is to fight against Satan; to rescue souls from the devil, especially at the hour of death; to attend the dying and accompany them to judgment; and to be the champion of God's people on earth and Patron of the Church.

I have great reverence for Saint Michael the Archangel; he had no example to follow in doing the will of God, and yet he fulfilled God's will faithfully. (667)

Prayer to St. Michael the Archangel

St. Michael the Archangel, defend us in battle; be our defense against the wickedness and snares of the devil. May God rebuke him, we humbly pray. And do you, O prince of the heavenly hosts, by the power of God, thrust into hell Satan and all the evil spirits, who prowl about the world seeking the ruin of souls. Amen.

Prayer to the Archangels

Heavenly King, You have given us archangels
to assist us during our pilgrimage on earth.

St. Michael is our protector;
I ask him to come to my aid,
fight for all my loved ones,
and protect us from danger.

St. Gabriel is a messenger of the Good News;
I ask him to help me
clearly hear Your voice
and to teach me the truth.

St. Raphael is the healing angel;
I ask him to take my need for healing
and that of everyone I know,
lift it up to Your throne of grace
and deliver back to us the gift of recovery.

Help us, O Lord,
to realize more fully the reality of the archangels
and their desire to serve us.
Holy angels,
pray for us. Amen.

Invocation to One's Holy Guardian Angel

Holy Angel, my counselor, inspire me.
Holy Angel, my defender, protect me.
Holy Angel, my faithful friend, intercede for me.
Holy Angel, my consoler, fortify me.
Holy Angel, my brother, defend me.
Holy Angel, my teacher, instruct me.
Holy Angel, witness of all my actions, purify me.
Holy Angel, my helper, support me.
Holy Angel, my intercessor, speak for me.
Holy Angel, my guide, direct me.
Holy Angel, my light, enlighten me.
Holy Angel, whom God has assigned to lead me, govern me.

(Translated from *Missal Romano Quotidiano* Edições Paulinas, São Paulo, 1959)

The Angel's Prayer at Fátima

When the Angel of Peace appeared to the three children at Fátima, he taught them to make acts of adoration to the Holy Trinity and to Jesus in the Blessed Sacrament in order to make reparation for sins and to give Glory to God.

O Most Holy Trinity, Father, Son, and Holy Spirit, I adore You profoundly. I offer You the most precious Body, Blood, Soul, and Divinity of Jesus Christ, present in all the tabernacles of the world, in reparation for outrages, sacrileges, and indifference of which He is offended. By the infinite merits of the Sacred Heart of Jesus and the Immaculate Heart of Mary, I beg conversion of poor sinners.

Most Holy Trinity, I adore You! My God, my God, I love You in the Most Blessed Sacrament!

"LET ALL MORTAL FLESH KEEP SILENCE"

"At His feet the six-winged seraph,
Cherubim with sleepless eye,
Veil their faces to the presence,
As with ceaseless voice they cry:
Alleluia, Alleluia,
Alleluia, Lord Most High!"

The Guardian Angel Prayer of St. Gertrude

O most holy Angel of God, appointed by God to be my guardian, I give you thanks for all the benefits which you have ever bestowed on me in body and in soul. I praise and glorify you that you condescended to assist me with such patient fidelity, and to defend me against all the assaults of my enemies. Blessed be the hour in which you were assigned me for my guardian, my defender and my patron. In acknowledgement and return for all your living ministries to me, I offer you the infinitely precious and noble heart of Jesus, and firmly purpose to obey you henceforward, and most faithfully to serve my God.

"When you pass before a chapel and do not have time to stop for a while, tell your Guardian Angel to carry out your errand to Our Lord in the tabernacle. He will accomplish it and then will still have time to catch up with you."

— ST. BERNADETTE
SOUBIROUS

XI. Adoration with the Saints

Let the [saints] exult in glory;
let them sing for joy on their couches.
— PSALM 149:5

Since apostolic times, a great devotion to Our Lord in the Eucharist has been a cornerstone of the lives of the saints. (And, of course, Faustina was no exception!)

And since the first century, when the faithful gathered to pray at the tombs of Christian martyrs, the practice of praying for and *with* our beloved dead has flourished. So, too, has the assurance that they're praying for us.

But in her diary, St. Faustina speaks of more than that: she tells of her own yearning to *become* a saint. And she invites each of us to become one too.

———

I understood how closely the three stages of a soul's life are bound together; that is to say, life on earth, in purgatory and in heaven [the Communion of Saints]. (594)

O dearest Treasure of my heart, I offer You all the adoration and thanksgiving of the Saints and of all the choirs of Angels.... (220)

My Jesus, You know that from my earliest years I have wanted to

"I rejoiced greatly at the fact of how much the saints think of us and of how closely we are united with them. Oh, the goodness of God! How beautiful is the spiritual world, that already here on earth we commune with the saints!" (448)

become a great saint; that is to say, I have wanted to love You with a love so great that there would be no soul who has hitherto loved You so. (1372)

Let no soul, even the most miserable, fall prey to doubt; for, as long as one is alive, each one can become a great saint, so great is the power of God's grace. It remains only for us not to oppose God's action. (283)

Prayers of the Saints

Prayer to Jesus in the Tabernacle
by St. Thérèse of Lisieux
(St. Faustina's favorite saint)

O God, hidden in the prison of the tabernacle! I come with joy to you each evening to thank you for the graces you have given me. I ask pardon for the faults I committed today, which just has slipped away like a dream....

O Jesus, how happy I would be if I had been faithful, but alas! Often in the evening I am sad because I feel I could have corresponded better with your graces.... If I were more united to you, more charitable, more humble, and more mortified, I would feel less sorrow when I talk with you in prayer.

And yet, O my God, very far from becoming discouraged at the sight of my miseries, I come to you with confidence, recalling that "those who are well do not need a doctor but the sick do." I beg you, then, to cure me and to pardon me. I will keep in mind, Lord, "that the soul to whom you have forgiven more should also love you more than the others!" ... I offer you every beat of my heart as so many acts of love and reparation, and I unite them to your infinite merits. I beg you, O my Divine Bridegroom, to be the Restorer of my soul, to act in me despite my resistance; and lastly, I wish to have no other will but yours. Tomorrow, with the help of your grace, I will begin a new life in which each moment will be an act of love and renunciation.

Thus, after coming each evening to the foot of your Altar, I will finally reach the last evening of my life. Then will begin for me the unending day of eternity when I will place in your Divine Heart the struggles of exile! Amen.

"During meditation, the Lord gave me knowledge of the joy of heaven and of the saints on our arrival there; they love God as the sole object of their love, but they also have a tender and heartfelt love for us. It is from the face of God that this joy flows, out upon all, because we see Him face to face. His face is so sweet that the soul falls anew into ecstasy." (1592)

Prayer to St. Mary Magdalene

Mary Magdalene — who, with the angels, was the first to adore the Risen Christ — help me never stop searching for my Lord, my Teacher, my Rabboni. Help me never stop listening for His calling my name. Help me never stop rushing to tell others what I've seen and heard, what I've come to believe. Amen.

Prayer of St. Gertrude the Great

I fall down before You with most profound reverence, O most Holy Sacrament, and with Angels and Archangels, with Thrones and Dominations, with Cherubim and Seraphim, and with all the glorious array of the heavenly host, I sing to Your glory, saying: Blessed a thousand, yes, ten thousand-fold, be the most Holy Sacrament of the Altar!

ST. JOHN BOSCO ON THE BLESSED SACRAMENT

"Do you want the Lord to give you many graces? Visit Him often. Do you want Him to give you few graces? Visit Him rarely. Do you want the devil to attack you? Visit Jesus rarely in the Blessed Sacrament. Do you want him to flee from you? Visit Jesus often. Do you want to conquer the devil? Take refuge often at the feet of Jesus. Do you want to be conquered by the devil? Forget about visiting Jesus. My dear ones, the visit to the Blessed Sacrament is an extremely necessary way to conquer the devil. Therefore, go often to visit Jesus and the devil will not come out victorious against you."

Prayer of St. Ignatius of Loyola

(The patron of St. Faustina's congregation and who appeared to her)

Take, O Lord, and receive all my liberty, my memory, my understanding, and my entire will, all that I have and possess. You have given all to me; to You, O Lord, I return it. All is Yours; dispose of it according to Your will. Give me Your love and Your grace, for this is enough for me.

St. Peter Julian Eymard: Pray Through St. Joseph

We have close to us as much as Joseph had at Nazareth; we have Our Lord in the Blessed Sacrament, but our poor eyes fail to see Him. Let us once become interior souls and we shall immediately see. In no better way can we enter into the Heart of Our Lord than through St. Joseph. Jesus and Mary are eager to pay the debts which they owe him for his devoted care of them, and their greatest pleasure is to fulfill his least desire. Let him, then, lead you by hand into the interior sanctuary of Jesus Eucharistic.

Prayer of St. Maximilian Kolbe

Who would dare to imagine that You, oh infinite, eternal God, have loved me for centuries, or to be more precise, from before the beginning of the centuries?

In fact, You have loved me ever since You have existed as God; thus, You have always loved me and You shall always love me!

… Your love for me was already there, even when I had no existence, and precisely because You loved me, oh good God, You called me from nothingness to existence!

… For me You have created the skies scattered with stars, for me the earth, the seas, the mountains, the streams, and all the beautiful things on earth….

Still, this did not satisfy You: to show me close up that You loved me so tenderly, You came down from the purest delights of heaven to this tarnished and tear-ridden world, You lived amidst poverty, hard work and suffering; and finally, despised and mocked, You let Yourself be suspended in torment on a vile scaffold between two criminals….

Oh God of love, You have redeemed me in this terrible, though generous, fashion!

… Who would venture to imagine it?

Yet, You were not satisfied with this. You knew that no fewer than nine-

teen centuries would still have to pass from the moment You poured out these demonstrations of Your love to the time I was to be born, so You decided to take care of this too!

Your Heart did not consent to let my only nourishment be the memories of Your boundless love.

You have remained on this forlorn planet in the holiest and most admirable Sacrament of the altar, and now You come to me and You closely unite Yourself to me under the appearance of food....

Now Your Blood flows in my blood; Your Soul, oh God incarnate, permeates my soul, giving it strength and nourishment....

What wonders!

Prayer of Blessed Charles de Foucauld

I am so near to You, so close to You, O my God. Let me serve You here in Your presence as I ought, give me such thoughts and words as I should have in You, by You and for You.

VENERABLE ARCHBISHOP FULTON SHEEN'S HOLY HOUR OF PRAYER

"The reason I keep up the Holy Hour is to grow more and more into his likeness. As Paul puts it: 'We are transfigured into his likeness, from splendor to splendor.' We become like that which we gaze upon. Looking into a sunset, the face takes on a golden glow. Looking at the Eucharistic Lord for an hour transforms the heart in a mysterious way as the face of Moses was transformed after his companionship with God on the mountain. Something happens to us similar to that which happened to the disciples at Emmaus. On Easter Sunday afternoon when the Lord met them, he asked why they were so gloomy. After spending some time in his presence, and hearing again the secret of spirituality — 'The Son of Man must suffer to enter into his Glory' — their time with him ended and their 'hearts were on fire.'

"… So the Holy Hour, quite apart from all its positive spiritual benefits, kept my feet from wandering too far. Being tethered to a tabernacle, one's rope for finding other pastures is not so long. That dim tabernacle lamp, however pale and faint, had some mysterious luminosity to darken the brightness of 'bright lights.' The Holy Hour became like an oxygen tank to revive the breath of the Holy Spirit in the midst of the foul and fetid atmosphere of the world. Even when it seemed so unprofitable and lacking in spiritual intimacy, I still had the sensation of being at least like a dog at the master's door, ready in case he called me."

XII. Prayers for Priests and Religious

"The harvest is plentiful, but the laborers are few; pray therefore
the Lord of the harvest to send out laborers into his harvest."
— MATTHEW 9:37–38

Time and again St. Faustina wrote of the strong, positive, and consoling impact priests had on her life. Knowing firsthand the blessings and challenges of living in a religious community, she was aware of both the power of members' prayers and, at the same time, their need for the prayers of others. A true daughter of Poland, St. Faustina always had the welfare of her country close to her heart.

———

A vision of the Mother of God. In the midst of a great brilliance, I saw the Mother of God clothed in a white gown, girt about with a golden cincture; and there were tiny stars, also of gold, over the whole garment, and chevron-shaped sleeves lined with gold. Her cloak was sky-blue, lightly thrown over the shoulders. A transparent veil was delicately drawn over her head, while her flowing hair was set off beautifully by a golden crown which terminated in little crosses. On Her left arm She held the Child Jesus. A Blessed Mother of this type I had not yet seen. Then She looked at me kindly and said: I am the Mother of God of Priests. At that, She lowered Jesus from her arm to the ground, raised Her right hand heavenward and said: O God, bless Poland, bless priests. (1585)

Dearest Mary, I join you in prayers for priests and for my country.

THE PRIESTHOOD NEEDS PRAYERS

"No words I can use would be too strong to state that the Catholic priesthood needs prayer and sacrifice as never before since Calvary. Priests experience pressures with a violence and a virulence such as no one else but a priest can understand. One saint after another has declared that the devil's principle target on earth is the Catholic priest. Priests need special graces from God. We ask, why pray, then, for priests? We should pray for priests and bishops because this has been the practice of the Church since apostolic times. It's a matter of truth. It is a divine mandate."

— Father John Hardon, S.J., "The Value of Prayer and Sacrifice for Priests," The Real Presence Association

O priests, you bright candles enlightening human souls, let your brightness never be dimmed. (75)

Holy Spirit, fill the minds and hearts of priests and religious with your wisdom.

I went at once before the Blessed Sacrament and offered myself with Jesus, present in the Most Holy Sacrament, to the Everlasting Father. Then I heard these words in my soul: ... I place in your care two pearls very precious to My Heart: these are the souls of priests and religious. You will pray particularly for them.... (531)

... I ask You for a special blessing and for light, O Jesus, for the priests.... (240)

Everlasting Father, give a special blessing and light to the souls of priests and religious.

Lent is a very special time for the work of priests. We should assist them in rescuing souls. (931)

St. Faustina, help me become better at making personal sacrifices as a way of praying for those who are ordained and those who have professed religious vows.

[St. Faustina prayed:] I desire sanctity for priests. (1581)

Dearest Lord, help our priests lead the lives to which you have called them.

O Jesus, give us fervent and holy priests! Oh, how great is the dignity of the priest, but at the same time, how great is his responsibility! Much has been given you, O priest, but much will also be demanded of you. (941)

Thank you, Dear Jesus, for those You have called and chosen. In the midst of the many demands of their ministry, let them always know Your peace.

A PRAYER FOR LABORERS FOR YOUR HARVEST

O God, You sent Your Son, Jesus, to bring eternal life to those who believe. I join Him in praying for laborers for Your harvest. May your Holy Spirit inspire men and women to continue His mission through Your priesthood, diaconate, religious life, and lay ministry. May this same Spirit make known Your will for my life. Amen.

February 15, 1937. Today my suffering increased somewhat: I not only feel greater pain all through my lungs, but also some strange pains in my intestines. I am suffering as much as my weak nature can bear, all for immortal souls, to plead the mercy of God for poor sinners and to beg for strength for priests. Oh, how much reverence I have for priests; and I am asking Jesus, the High Priest, to grant them many graces. (953)

Today, Lord, I offer up my worries, my heartaches, and my pains as a prayer for the holy souls in purgatory, especially for priests.

A PRAYER FOR PRIESTLY VOCATIONS

Lord Jesus Christ, / you promised always to give your Church shepherds. / In faith, we know your promise cannot fail. / Trusting in the power of the Holy Spirit at work in the Church, / we pray you raise up sacred ministers from your holy people, / that the Sacrifice in which you give your Body and Blood / may be daily renewed in the world until we come to that Kingdom / where you live with the Father and the Holy Spirit, / one God, for ever and ever. Amen.

— "A Holy Hour of Prayer for Vocations,"
United States Conference of Catholic Bishops

… The Lord gave me knowledge of His anger toward mankind which deserves to have its days shortened because of its sins. But I learned that the world's existence is maintained by chosen souls; that is, the religious orders. Woe to the world when there will be a lack of religious orders! (1434)

[Jesus said to St. Faustina:] In convents too, there are souls that fill my heart with joy.... They are a defense for the world before the justice of the Heavenly Father and a means of obtaining mercy for the world. The love and sacrifice of these souls sustain the world in existence. (367)

Thank you, Almighty God, for the members of religious orders who never cease praying for all of us, who never cease praying for me.

XIII. Adoration for the Dying and the Holy Souls in Purgatory

He will wipe away every tear from their
eyes, and death shall be no more.
— REVELATION 21:4

Through her times at Mass and reception of Holy Communion; through her prayers, devotions, meditations, and acts of adoration — through her personal suffering and sacrifices — St. Faustina's life in the convent was an unending string of petitions to Divine Mercy for others, including, in a special way, the dying and the holy souls in purgatory.

Adoring for the Dying

The fifty-third footnote in St. Faustina's diary explains:

All Sisters devote one day at the beginning of the month to spiritual renewal, the so-called one-day retreat. There is no recreation on that day. The Sisters keep silence and have an hour of meditation, the Way of the Cross, monthly examination of conscience, and a half hour meditation about death.

—

O my Jesus, Life of my soul, my Life, my Savior, my sweetest Bridegroom, and at the same time my Judge, You know that in this last hour of mine I do not count on any merits of my own, but only on Your mercy. Even as of today, I immerse myself totally in the abyss of Your mercy, which is always open to every soul. (1553)

During one of the adorations, Jesus promised me that: With souls that have recourse to My mercy and with those that glorify and proclaim My great mercy to others, I will deal according to My infinite mercy at the hour of their death....

Remember My Passion, and if you do not believe My words, at least believe My wounds. (379)

Jesus, hide me in Your mercy and shield me against everything that might terrify my soul. Do not let my trust in Your mercy be disappointed. Shield me with the omnipotence of Your mercy, and judge me leniently as well. (1480)

O merciful Jesus, stretched on the cross, be mindful of the hour of our death. O most merciful Heart of Jesus, opened with a lance, shelter me at the last moment of my life. (813)

O hidden Jesus, in the many struggles of my last hour,
May the omnipotence of Your grace be poured out upon my soul,
That at death's moment I may gaze upon You
And see You face to face, as do the chosen in heaven. (1479)

HOW TO PRAY THE CHAPLET OF DIVINE MERCY

On Rosary beads begin:

Our Father, Hail Mary, the Apostles' Creed.

On the Our Father beads, pray:

Eternal Father, I offer You the Body and Blood, Soul and Divinity of Your dearly Beloved Son, Our Lord Jesus Christ, in atonement for our sins and those of the whole world.

On the Hail Mary beads, pray:

For the sake of His sorrowful Passion, have mercy on us and on the whole world.

In conclusion, pray three times:

Holy God, Holy Mighty One, Holy Immortal One, have mercy on us and on the whole world.

Jesus listened to these outpourings of my heart with gravity and interest, as if He had known nothing about them, and this seemed to make it easier for me to talk. And the Lord said to me, My daughter, those words of your heart are pleasing to Me, and by saying the chaplet you are bringing humankind closer to Me. After these words, I found myself alone, but the presence of God is always in my soul. (929)

The Lord's Promise: The souls that say this chaplet will be embraced by My mercy during their lifetime and especially at the hour of their death. (754)

When I entered my solitude, I heard these words: *[Jesus said:]* At the hour of their death, I defend as My own glory every soul that will say this chaplet; or when others say it for a dying person, the pardon is the same. When this chaplet is said by the bedside of a dying person, God's anger is placated, unfathomable mercy envelops the soul, and the very depths of My tender mercy are moved for the sake of the sorrowful Passion of My Son.

Oh, if only everyone realized how great the Lord's mercy is and how much we all need that mercy, especially at that crucial hour! (811)

[Jesus said to St. Faustina:] My daughter, encourage souls to say the chaplet which I have given to you. It pleases Me to grant everything they ask of Me by saying the chaplet. When hardened sinners say it, I will fill their souls with peace, and the hour of their death will be a happy one. (1541)

O Christ, I am most delighted when I see that You are loved, and that Your praise and glory resound, especially the praise of Your mercy. O Christ, to the last moment of my life, I will not stop glorifying Your goodness and mercy. With every drop of my blood, with every beat of my heart, I glorify Your mercy. I long to be entirely transformed into a hymn of Your glory. When I find myself on my deathbed, may the last beat of my heart be a loving hymn in praise of Your unfathomable mercy. (1708)

Prayers for the Dying

O most merciful Jesus,
Lover of souls, I pray You
by the agony of Your most Sacred Heart,
and by the sorrows of Your Immaculate Mother,
wash in Your Blood the sinners of this whole world
who are now in their last agony, and are to die this day. Amen.

O heart of Jesus, once in agony, pity the dying!

Prayer to St. Mary Magdalene

Good Jesus, St. Mary Magdalene was one of the women who assisted You and the apostles during Your public ministry. She cried with the Blessed Mother and St. John at the foot of your Cross, and she helped to bury Your dead body.

For serving You with such devotion, she was the first to see You resurrected. I ask her to pray for me when I have opportunities to assist others as they approach death or grieve the death of loved ones. Inspire me, O God, in giving them Your comfort, in helping them accept salvation, and in guiding the survivors to release their loved ones into Your arms.

St. Mary Magdalene, pray for us.

St. Faustina prayed to Our Lady of Perpetual Help and taught this prayer to the Novices: "Mother of Perpetual Help, I approach you as my Mother in all the suffering that assail me and in very need of my life. Therefore, at any time of day or night come to the aid of my helplessness and in the hour of my death come to my aid, my only Mother."

Consecration to the Most Chaste Heart of St. Joseph

We are called to pray for a happy death (to die in the state of grace) for ourselves, families, and those near death. Go to Joseph! He is the patron of a happy death. He died in the arms of Jesus and Mary.

———

St. Joseph, you accepted your mission from God: to be the husband of Mary and the foster father and guardian of Jesus. In the home at Nazareth and your most chaste heart, there was no place for sin. Help us to imitate that purity of heart and act with resolve like you, when God calls. May the power of grace transform us to accept the reign of Christ in our own hearts.

Inspire in us a strong devotion to your most chaste heart. In doing so, you promise to safeguard us in this life and console and defend us at the moment of death.

St. Joseph, we trust in your intercession. You wait silently, always at hand and pleased to assist those who dedicate themselves to you. And at the end of our lives, may we enjoy and share your most privileged intimacy with Our Lady and the Blessed Trinity in heaven. Amen.

(Mother Marie André, PCPA, Abbess of Our Lady of Solitude Monastery)

Adoring for the Holy Souls in Purgatory

With every Mass, with every act of adoration before the Blessed Sacrament, we decrease our time in purgatory. Through those actions, through our prayers and sacrifices, we can decrease the time of souls who are there now. Souls who are praying for us now.

———

Before All Souls' Day, I went to the cemetery at dusk. Although it was locked, I managed to open the gate a bit and said, "If you need something, my dear little souls, I will be glad to help you to the extent that the rule permits me." I then heard these words, "Do the will of God; we are happy in the measure that we have fulfilled God's will." (518)

In the evening, these souls came and asked me to pray for them, and I did pray very much for them. In the evening, when the procession was returning from the cemetery, I saw a great multitude of souls walking with us into the chapel and praying with us. I prayed a good deal, for I had my superiors' permission to do so. (519)

I saw Our Lady visiting the souls in Purgatory. The souls call her "The Star of the Sea." She brings them refreshment. I wanted to talk with them some more, but my Guardian Angel beckoned me to leave. We went out of that prison of suffering. [I heard an interior voice] which said, My mercy does not want this, but justice demands it. Since that time, I am in closer communion with the suffering souls. (20)

"Star of the Stormy Sea of my mortal life, may your light guide me so I do not stray from the path that leads me to heaven!"

O terrible hour, at which one is obliged to see all one's deeds in their nakedness and misery; not one of them is lost, they will all accompany us to God's judgment. I can find no words or comparisons to express such terrible things. And although it seems to me that this soul is not damned, nevertheless its torments are in no way different from the torments of hell; there is only this difference: that they will someday come to an end. (426)

When the soul of a certain young lady came to me one night, she made me aware of her presence, and made known to me that she needed my prayer. I prayed for a while, but her spirit did not leave me. Then I thought to myself, "If you are a good spirit, leave me in peace, and the indulgences I will gain tomorrow will be for you." At that moment, the spirit left my room, and I recognized that she was in purgatory. (1723)

But towards evening I felt very exhausted and could not make my Holy Hour, so I asked Mother Superior to allow me to go to bed early. I fell asleep as soon as I lay down, but at about eleven o'clock Satan shook my bed. I awoke instantly, and I started to pray peacefully to my Guardian Angel. Then I saw the souls who were doing penance in purgatory. They appeared like shadows.... (412)

O merciful God, You do not despise us, but lavish Your graces on us continuously. You make us fit to enter Your kingdom.... (1339)

On one occasion, when I dropped by the chapel for a five-minute adoration and was praying for a certain soul, I came to understand that God does not always accept our petitions for the souls we have in mind, but directs these to other souls. Hence, although we do not relieve the souls we intended to relieve in their purgatorial suffering, still our prayer is not lost. (621)

In the evening after Vespers, I went to the cemetery [in the sisters' park]. I had been praying for a while when I saw one of our sisters, who said to me, "We are in the chapel." I understood that I was to go to the chapel and there pray and gain the indulgences. The next day, during Holy Mass, I saw three white doves soaring from the altar toward heaven. I understood that not only the three souls that I saw had gone to heaven, but also many others who had died beyond the confines of our institute. Oh, how good and merciful is the Lord! (748)

When I entered the chapel for a moment in the evening, I felt a terrible thorn in my head. This lasted for a short time, but the pricking was so painful that in an instant my head dropped onto the communion rail. It seemed to me that the thorn had thrust itself into my brain. But all this is nothing; it is all for the sake of souls, to obtain God's mercy for them. (1399)

Prayers for the Holy Souls in Purgatory

Eternal rest grant unto them, O Lord. And let perpetual light shine upon them. May they rest in peace. Amen.

May their souls and the souls of all the faithful departed, through the mercy of God, rest in peace. Amen.

———

O Lord through your Divine mercy, your love and compassion, please welcome into your Sacred Heart, your loving arms, and your heavenly home the holy souls in purgatory, that they may attain their eternal peace and happiness with you, their Lord and Savior. Amen.

———

O Eternal Father, I offer you through the Immaculate Virgin Mary, the Precious Blood of your Son, for the relief of the suffering souls in purgatory. Amen.

———

My Jesus, by the sorrows you suffered in your agony in the garden,
In the scourging and crowning with thorns,
In the way to Calvary,
In your crucifixion and death,
Have mercy on the souls in purgatory.
Especially those who are most forsaken.
Deliver them from the dire torments they endure,
And admit them to your most sweet embrace in paradise. Amen.

Prayer to St. Nicholas of Tolentino, Patron of the Holy Souls in Purgatory

God, you are the Father of mercy towards those who have been redeemed by the Blood of your Son Jesus, and have given us St. Nicholas of Tolentino as special intercessor for the dead. Hear my prayer which I make to you with all confidence for my beloved whom you have called to yourself.

St. Nicholas, you were moved with compassion by the sorrowful pleas of the souls who in their suffering appeared to you in a vision, begging your prayers. Intercede for the dead who are still in need of help, especially my dear ones. Hasten with your help an end to their purification and thus their joyous meeting with God in the plentitude of the glory of the blessed.

And you, Holy Souls, come to my help in times of difficulty and preserve me from all danger. Amen.

Prayer for Souls,
Attributed to St. Gertrude

Eternal Father, I offer you the Most Precious Blood of your Divine Son, Jesus, in union with the Masses said throughout the world today, for all the holy souls in purgatory, for sinners everywhere, for sinners in the universal Church, those in my own home and within my family. Amen.

Act of Mercy for the Holy Souls

Immaculate Mary, Mother of Mercy, who saw the sacred body of your beloved Son raised on the Cross, looked at the soil soaked with his Blood, and were present at his cruel death, we offer you, most Holy Mother, the souls suffering in purgatory, and we beg you to be kind as to look upon them with your merciful eyes and ask for their release from their torments. Amen.

XIV. Spiritual Adoration at Home

Hear, O LORD, when I cry aloud,
be gracious to me and answer me!
Thou hast said, "Seek ye my face."
My heart says to thee,
"Thy face, LORD, do I seek."
Hide not thy face from me.
— PSALM 27:7–9

[Jesus said:] You can come to me at any moment, at any time; I want to speak to you and desire to grant you grace. (1485)

—

It can be helpful — and comforting — to keep in mind that St. Faustina wasn't always in the chapel, wasn't always before Our Lord in the Eucharist, when she offered adoration.

There were times when her fragile health, and later her terminal condition, made it impossible for her leave her room or even her bed. On those occasions, she would spiritually "take flight" to make her acts of adoration.

Yes, when the term "adoration" is used today, what's usually meant is visiting a church and spending time before the tabernacle. Stopping in at a Eucharistic chapel for a visit or holy hour. Attending Benediction.

But in the same way that you can make a "spiritual communion" when you're unable to get to Mass, you can make a "spiritual adoration" — anywhere, anytime.

LIVING FAITH

St. Faustina's devotion to the Eucharist was an act of living faith. She lived by faith and love. Because of this, she felt the need to be with Jesus even when she was unable to.

When I steeped myself in prayer, I was transported in spirit to the chapel, where I saw the Lord Jesus, exposed in the monstrance. In place of the monstrance, I saw the glorious face of the Lord, and He said to me, What you see in reality, these souls see through faith. Oh, how pleasing to Me is their great faith! You see, although there appears to be no trace of life in Me, in reality it is present in its fullness in each and every Host. But for Me to be able to act upon a soul, the soul must have faith. O how pleasing to Me is living faith! (1420)

In a particular and miraculous way, Jesus is present in the Eucharist, but He, the Father, and the Holy Spirit are always with you. Always.

And God knows that you can have very good reasons and obligations for not visiting Him in a church or chapel. It may be your health or the health of a loved one you're caring for. It may be your family responsibilities or your job. It may be the distance to that church or chapel. It may be that it's the middle of the night, you've just woken up, and can't get back to sleep, but you want to take a moment or two to adore Him. To praise Him. To deliberately acknowledge His presence with you and your love for Him.

You can do that in your bed. From your sofa or wheelchair. In your car. At work. On a walk. Waiting in line.

You can do that with the prayers and songs of others, including St. Faustina. In the psalms that were written so long ago. Or in your own words.

From your own heart. A prayer that can be as simple as lovingly repeating, "I adore you." A prayer that can be wordless. God knows.

———

When night fell, the physical sufferings increased and were joined by moral sufferings. Night and suffering. The solemn silence of the night made it possible for me to suffer freely. My body was stretched on the wood of the cross. I writhed in terrible pain until eleven o'clock. I went in spirit to the Tabernacle and uncovered the ciborium, leaning my head on the rim of the cup, and all my tears flowed silently toward the Heart of Him who alone understands what pain and suffering is. And I experienced the sweetness of this suffering, and my soul came to desire this sweet agony, which I would not have exchanged for all the world's treasures. The Lord gave me strength of spirit and love towards those through whom these sufferings came. (1454)

Now that I have difficulty sleeping at night, because my suffering won't allow it, I *[spiritually]* visit all the churches and chapels and, if only for a brief moment, I make an act of adoration before the Blessed Sacrament. When I return to my chapel, I then pray for certain priests who proclaim and glory The Divine Mercy. I also pray for the intentions of the Holy Father and to obtain mercy for sinners — such are my nights. (1501)

Making a Spiritual Communion

In his encyclical *Ecclesia de Eucharistia* ("The Church from the Eucharist") of April 2003, St. John Paul II encouraged the practice of spiritual communion, "which has happily been established in the Church for centuries and recommended by saints who were masters of the spiritual life" (n. 34).

St. Thomas Aquinas described it as "an ardent desire to receive Jesus in the most holy sacrament and lovingly embrace him" at a time or in circumstances when we cannot receive Him in sacramental Communion.

Spiritual Communion Prayer

O Jesus I turn toward the holy tabernacle where you live hidden for love of me. I love you, O my God. I cannot receive you in Holy Communion. Come nevertheless and visit me with your grace. Come spiritually into my heart. Purify it. Sanctify it. Render it like unto your own. Amen.

Short Prayers of Adoration

O Jesus in the Blessed Sacrament, have mercy on us!

———

Praise and adoration ever more be given to the most holy Sacrament.

———

O Sacrament most holy, O Sacrament divine! All praise and all thanksgiving be every moment Thine!

THE "SPIRITUAL ADORATION" OF THREE SAINTS

St. Stanislaus Kostka (1550–1568) took every free moment to visit the Blessed Sacrament. When he could not make it, he would turn to his guardian angel and say: "My dear angel, go there for me."

———

Portuguese mystic and victim soul **Blessed Alexandrina Maria da Costa** (1904–1955) was bedridden for many years but would make "flights" in her heart to visit tabernacles around the world.

———

St. Pio of Pietrelcina (1887–1968) gave this counsel to one of his spiritual daughters:

> In the course of the day, when it is not permitted to you to do otherwise, call Jesus, even in the midst of all your occupations, with a resigned sigh of the soul and He will come and will remain always united with your soul by means of His grace and His holy love. Make a spiritual flight before the Tabernacle, when you cannot go there with your body, and there pour out the ardent desires of your spirit and embrace the Beloved of souls ... better than if it had been permitted to you to receive Him sacramentally.

The Nicene Creed Litany of Adoration

I believe in and adore one God.

Father almighty, maker of heaven and earth, of all things visible and invisible,
I adore you.

Lord Jesus Christ, the Only Begotten Son of God, born of the Father before
all ages,
I adore you.

God from God, Light from Light, true God from true God, begotten, not
made, consubstantial with the Father,
I adore you.

Through you all things were made.
I adore you.

For me and for my salvation you came down from heaven, and by the Holy
Spirit were incarnate of the Virgin Mary, and became man.
I adore you.

For my sake you were crucified under Pontius Pilate, suffered death and
were buried, and rose again on the third day in accordance with the Scriptures.
I adore you.

You ascended into heaven and are seated at the right hand of the Father.
I adore you.

You will come again in glory to judge the living and the dead and your
kingdom will have no end.
I adore you.

Holy Spirit, the Lord, the giver of life, who proceeds from the Father and the Son,
I adore you.

Holy Spirit, who with the Father and the Son is adored and glorified, who has spoken through the prophets,
I adore you.

Triune God, I believe in one, holy, catholic, and apostolic Church.
I adore you.

Triune God, I confess one Baptism for the forgiveness of sins.
I adore you.

Triune God, I look forward to the resurrection of the dead and the life of the world to come.
I adore you.

Adoration be to the Father, and to the Son, and to the Holy Spirit. As it was in the beginning, is now, and ever shall be, world without end. Amen.

Te Deum

The *Te Deum* is a moving tribute to God in His triune majesty. The hymn combines important elements of prayer to God, including adoration, supplication, and thanksgiving. The Church triumphant (those in heaven) and the Church militant (those on earth) sing God's praises in adoration in this hymn.

You are God: we praise you;
You are the Lord: we acclaim you;

You are the eternal Father:
All creation worships you.

To you all angels, all the powers of heaven,
Cherubim and Seraphim, sing in endless praise:
  Holy, holy, holy, Lord, God of power and might,
  heaven and earth are full of your glory.

The glorious company of apostles praise you.
The noble fellowship of prophets praise you.
The white-robed army of martyrs praise you.

Throughout the world the holy Church acclaims you:
  Father, of majesty unbounded,
  your true and only Son, worthy of all worship,
  and the Holy Spirit, advocate and guide.

You, Christ, are the king of glory,
the eternal Son of the Father.

When you became man to set us free
you did not spurn the Virgin's womb.

You overcame the sting of death,
and opened the kingdom of heaven to all believers.

You are seated at God's right hand in glory.
We believe that you will come, and be our judge.

Come then, Lord, and help your people,
bought with the price of your own blood,
and bring us with your saints
to glory everlasting.

Praying with the Psalms

When our minds are empty or distracted, we can turn to the Book of Psalms to focus our prayer. These inspired words can be the perfect expression of what we want to say to God. This compilation of the psalms is designed to help us express the sentiments and needs of our souls.

ADORATION PRAYER BY KING DAVID

"Thine, O Lord, is the greatness, and the power, and the glory, and the victory, and the majesty; for all that is in the heavens and in the earth is thine; thine is the kingdom, O Lord, and thou art exalted as head above all. Both riches and honor come from thee, and thou rulest over all. In thy hand are power and might; and in thy hand it is to make great and to give strength to all."

— 1 Chronicles 29:11–12

Praise You, Lord
Praise the Lord!
Praise the Lord from the heavens,
    praise him in the heights!
Praise him, all his angels,
    praise him, all his host!

Praise him, sun and moon,
    praise him, all you shining stars!
Praise him, you highest heavens,
    and you waters above the heavens!

Let them praise the name of the LORD!
    For he commanded and they were created.
And he established them for ever and ever;
    he fixed their bounds which cannot be passed.

Praise the LORD from the earth,
    you sea monsters and all deeps,
fire and hail, snow and frost,
    stormy wind fulfilling his command!

Mountains and all hills,
    fruit trees and all cedars!
Beasts and all cattle,
    creeping things and flying birds!

Kings of the earth and all peoples,
    princes and all rulers of the earth!
Young men and maidens together,
    old men and children!

Let them praise the name of the LORD,
    for his name alone is exalted;
    his glory is above earth and heaven.
He has raised up a horn for his people,
    praise for all his saints,
    for the people of Israel who are near to him.
Praise the LORD! (Ps 148)

Thank You, Lord
I will give thanks to the LORD with my whole heart;
    I will tell of all thy wonderful deeds.

I will be glad and exult in thee;
>
> I will sing praise to thy name, O Most High. (Ps 9:1–2)

I will give thanks to thee, O Lord, among the peoples;
>
> I will sing praises to thee among the nations.

For thy steadfast love is great to the heavens,
>
> thy faithfulness to the clouds. (Ps 57:9–10)

Please Listen to Me, Lord

To thee, O Lord, I call;
>
> my rock, be not deaf to me....

Hear the voice of my supplication,
>
> as I cry to thee for help,

as I lift up my hands
>
> toward thy most holy sanctuary. (Ps 28:1–2)

Hear, O Lord, when I cry aloud,
>
> be gracious to me and answer me!

Thou hast said, "Seek ye my face."
>
> My heart says to thee,

"Thy face, Lord, do I seek."
>
> Hide not thy face from me. (Ps 27:7–9)

Forgive Me, Lord

For thy name's sake, O Lord,
>
> pardon my guilt, for it is great....

Consider my affliction and my trouble,
>
> and forgive all my sins. (Ps 25:11, 18)

Have mercy on me, O God,
>
> according to thy steadfast love;

according to thy abundant mercy blot out
   my transgressions.
Wash me thoroughly from my iniquity,
   and cleanse me from my sin!

For I know my transgressions,
   and my sin is ever before me....
   [W]ash me, and I shall be whiter than snow. (Ps 51:1–3, 7)

Help Me Hear You, Lord

Let me hear what God the LORD will speak,
   for he will speak peace to his people,
to his saints, to those who turn to him in their hearts. (Ps 85:8)

With my whole heart I seek thee;
   let me not wander from thy commandments!
I have laid up thy word in my heart,
   that I might not sin against thee....

My soul melts away for sorrow;
   strengthen me according to thy word!...

How sweet are thy words to my taste,
   sweeter than honey to my mouth!...

Thy word is a lamp to my feet
   and a light to my path....

The unfolding of thy words gives light;
   it imparts understanding to the simple. (Ps 119:10–11, 28, 103,
      105, 130)

I'm Afraid, Lord

O LORD, how many are my foes!...
But thou, O LORD, art a shield about me,
    my glory, and the lifter of my head.
I cry aloud to the LORD,
    and he answers me from his holy hill.

I lie down and sleep;
    I wake again, for the LORD sustains me.
I am not afraid of ten thousands of people
    who have set themselves against me round about.

Arise, O LORD!
    Deliver me, O my God! (Ps 3:1, 3–7)

In peace I will both lie down and sleep;
    for thou alone, O LORD, makest me dwell in safety. (Ps 4:8)

But I trust in thee, O LORD;
    I say, "Thou art my God."
My times are in thy hand;
    deliver me from the hand of my enemies and persecutors!
        (Ps 31:14–15)

Protect Me and Give Me Courage, Lord

The LORD is my light and my salvation;
    whom shall I fear?
The LORD is the stronghold of my life;
    of whom shall I be afraid?

When evildoers assail me,
    uttering slanders against me,

my adversaries and foes,
    they shall stumble and fall.

Though a host encamp against me,
    my heart shall not fear;
though war arise against me,
    yet I will be confident.

For he will hide me in his shelter
    in the day of trouble;
he will conceal me under the cover of his tent,
    he will set me high upon a rock....

I believe that I shall see the goodness of the LORD
    in the land of the living!
Wait for the LORD;
    be strong, and let your heart take courage;
    yea, wait for the LORD! (Ps 27:1-3, 5, 13–14)

I Know You Watch over Me, Lord

The LORD is my shepherd, I shall not want;
    he makes me lie down in green pastures.
He leads me beside still waters;
    he restores my soul.
He leads me in paths of righteousness
    for his name's sake.

Even though I walk through the valley of the shadow
    of death,
    I fear no evil;

for thou art with me;
    thy rod and thy staff,
    they comfort me.

Thou preparest a table before me
    in the presence of my enemies;
thou anointest my head with oil,
    my cup overflows.
Surely goodness and mercy shall follow me all the days of my life;
and I shall dwell in the house of the LORD
    for ever. (Ps 23)

I Love You, Lord
I love thee, O LORD, my strength....

He brought me forth into a broad place;
    he delivered me, because he delighted in me....

The LORD lives; and blessed be my rock,
    and exalted be the God of my salvation. (Ps 18:1, 19, 46)

You Are So Kind to Me, Lord
The LORD is gracious and merciful,
    slow to anger and abounding in steadfast love.
The LORD is good to all,
    and his compassion is over all that he has made.

The LORD is faithful in all his words,
    and gracious in all his deeds.
The LORD upholds all who are falling,
    and raises up all who are bowed down.

The LORD is near to all who call upon him,
    to all who call upon him in truth.
He fulfills the desire of all who fear him,
    he also hears their cry, and saves them.
        (Ps 145:8–9, 13–14, 18–19)

For the Holy Souls in Purgatory, Lord
Out of the depths I cry to thee, O LORD!
    Lord, hear my voice!
Let thy ears be attentive
    to the voice of my supplications!

If thou, O LORD, shouldst mark iniquities,
    Lord, who could stand?
But there is forgiveness with thee....

I wait for the LORD, my soul waits,
    and in his word I hope....

    For with the LORD there is steadfast love,
    and with him is plenteous redemption.
And he will redeem Israel
    from all his iniquities. (Ps 130:1–5, 7–8)

Do not remember against us the iniquities of our forefathers;
    let thy compassion come speedily to meet us,
    for we are brought very low.
Help us, O God of our salvation,
    for the glory of thy name;
deliver us, and forgive our sins
    for thy name's sake! (Ps 79:8–9)

Bring me out of prison,
    that I may give thanks to thy name!
The righteous will surround me;
    for thou wilt deal bountifully with me. (Ps 142:7)

Blessings on Them All, Lord

May the Lord guide our religious leaders and communities, "giving them life, and making them blessed upon the earth, and delivering them not into the hands of their enemies."

May the Lord protect our political leaders and government workers, "not letting the enemy prevail over them nor iniquity have power to hurt them."

May the Lord save our nation with all its peoples, "blessing its inheritance and ruling over all its peoples as one."

May the Lord bless all our family and friends, "guarding their coming in and going out as well as helping them and their families to survive and prosper."

May the Lord look upon all the troubled and the poor, especially "their sufferings and earnest petitions," and swiftly enable human and material resources effectively to "attend to the misery of the needy and the groans of the poor" and "to deliver them from their troubles and grief" as well as "setting them in safety from all evil."

Help us know, O Lord, that your "promises are pure," that you "protect us and guard us forever," and that you "will place us in the safety for which we long." (See Ps 51, 20, 89, 21, 28, 20, 121, 125, 114, 41, 10, 12)

XV. Prayers for Various Intentions

I urge that supplications, prayers, intercessions,
and thanksgivings be made for all men....
— 1 TIMOTHY 2:1

When considering how to make a choice or decision, St. Faustina advised: "God looks at the intention with which we begin, and will reward us accordingly" (800).

It seems safe to say that, in a similar way, no doubt He listens to the particular intention of our prayer and will reward others accordingly (and us too).

For My Family

From nine to ten o'clock I offered my adoration for my parents and my whole family. (346)

My Dearest Jesus, I pray for my family and, today, especially for (mention names and intentions here).

For My Country

Dear Lord, I join St. Faustina in praying: Most merciful Jesus, I beseech You through the intercession of Your saints — and especially the intercession of Your dearest Mother, who nurtured You from childhood — bless my native land and bless the country in which I live now.

For Beloved Friends

Before supper, I went into the chapel for a moment to break the wafer spiritually with those beloved persons, so dear to my heart, though far away. First, I steeped myself in a profound prayer and asked the Lord for graces for them all as a group and then for each one individually. Jesus gave me to know how much this pleased Him, and my soul was filled with even greater joy to see that God loves in a special way those whom we love. (1438)

Thank you, Lord, for the many friends who have graced my life. What joys they've been and are to me! Today, I pray particularly for (mention names here).

For Those Who Asked Me to Pray for Them

One of the sisters had asked me to offer an hour of adoration for her. (355)

Heavenly Father, I'm praying today especially for (mention names here), who have asked me for prayers. Ease their minds and lighten their burdens. Give them what they ask for — but if that's not what's best for them, help them to accept Your will.

For the Sick and Suffering

I steeped myself in prayer, especially for the sick. I now see how much the sick have need of prayer. (826)

Gentle Father, be with those who are sick, elderly, disabled, or frail. Beloved St. John the Caregiver, pray for those who take care of them.

For the Mentally Ill and Those Considering Suicide

Once, I took upon myself a terrible temptation which one of our students in the house at Warsaw was going through. It was the temptation of suicide. For seven days I suffered; and after the seven days Jesus granted her the grace which was being asked, and then my suffering also ceased. It was a great suffering. (192)

Jesus, the Great Healer, bring comfort and peace to those who are mentally ill, including those who suffer from depression. Bless their loved ones and the health professionals who offer them care.

For Those Who Have Lost Hope in God's Mercy

I made my hour of adoration from eleven o'clock till midnight. I offered it for the conversion of hardened sinners, especially for those who have lost hope in God's mercy. (319)

Immaculate Heart of Mary, be with those whose hearts have been hardened by sin. Our Lady of Hope, pray for those who feel hopeless and are uncertain of your Son's mercy.

For the Conversion of Sinners

I offered the second hour of adoration for the conversion of sinners, and I tried especially to offer expiation to God for the insults that were being committed against Him at this present moment. (355)

Forgive them, Father, though some do know what they do.

For Those Whose Soul Is "Withering"

O Jesus, my Jesus, with what great pain is my soul pierced when I see this fountain of life gushing forth with such sweetness and power for each soul, while at the same time I see souls withering away and drying up through their own fault. O Jesus, grant that the power of mercy embrace these souls. (914)

Blessed Vine, give nourishment and new life to the branches who are spiritually dying.

For Spiritual Directors

From ten to eleven, I offered it for the intention of my spiritual director, in the first place thanking God for granting me this great visible help here on earth, just as He had promised me, and I also asked God to grant him the necessary light so that he could get to know my soul and guide me according to God's good pleasure. (346)

Holy Spirit, give your great wisdom to those You've chosen to help direct the minds, the hearts, and the souls of others.

For the Church, Missions, and Other Intentions

From eleven to twelve I prayed for the Holy Church and the clergy, for sinners, for the missions, and for our houses. I offered the indulgences for the souls in purgatory. (346)

For so many intentions — Dear God! — I should have written them down. But You know them even when I can't remember.

For Myself

Jesus make my heart like unto Yours, or rather transform it into Your own Heart that I may sense the needs of other hearts, especially those who are sad and suffering. May the rays of mercy rest in my heart. (514)

Jesus meek and humble of heart, help me love others as You do.

For Mercy on Me

Jesus, have mercy on me; do not entrust such great things to me, as You see that I am a bit of dust and completely inept. (53)

I know Your ways are not my ways, Lord, but I trust in You.

"When, during adoration, I repeated the prayer, 'Holy God' several times, a vivid presence of God suddenly swept over me, and I was caught up in spirit before the majesty of God. I saw how the Angels and the Saints of the Lord give glory to God. The glory of God is so great that I dare not try to describe it, because I would not be able to do so, and souls might think that what I have written is all there is. Saint Paul, I understand now why you did not want to describe heaven, but only said that eye has not seen, nor ear heard, nor has it entered into the heart of man what God has prepared for those who love Him [cf. 1 Cor 2:9; 2 Cor 12:1–7]." (1604)

Appendix

St. Faustina's Seven Insights on Adoration

Yes, St. Faustina's description of her time spent before the Lord in the Blessed Sacrament could fall into the four basic forms of prayer: adoration, petition, intercession, and thanksgiving. Yes, it could be a primer on the theological virtues of faith, hope, and charity.

But at its core, at its heart, it's a young nun opening *her* heart to her one, true Love. It's talking to Him about *everything* and listening to what He has to say. And, most beautifully, it's sitting in a mutual, comfortable, and comforting silence. It's being in the presence of God.

First Insight

I spend every free moment at the feet of the hidden God. He is my Master; I ask Him about everything; I speak to Him about everything. Here I obtain strength and light; here I learn everything; here I am given light on how to act toward my neighbor. From the time I left the novitiate, I have enclosed myself in the tabernacle together with Jesus, my Master. He Himself drew me into the fire of living love on which everything converges. (704)

Second Insight

It is no great thing to love God in prosperity / And thank Him when all goes well, / But rather to adore Him midst great adversities / And love Him for His own sake and place one's hope in Him. (995)

Third Insight

I thank God for this illness and these physical discomforts, because I have time to converse with the Lord Jesus. It is my delight to spend long hours at the feet of the hidden God, and the hours pass like minutes as I lose track of time. I feel that a fire is burning within me, and I understand no other life but that of sacrifice, which flows from pure love. (784)

I made an hour of adoration in thanksgiving for the graces which had been granted me and for my illness. Illness also is a great grace. (1062)

Fourth Insight

To suffer without complaining, to bring comfort to others and to drown my own sufferings in the most Sacred Heart of Jesus!

I will spend all my free moments at the feet of [Our Lord in] the Blessed Sacrament. At the feet of Jesus, I will seek light, comfort and strength. I will show my gratitude unceasingly to God for His great mercy towards me, never forgetting the favors He has bestowed on me. (224)

Fifth Insight

If only souls would become recollected, God would speak to them at once, for dissipation drowns out the word of the Lord. (452)

Sixth Insight

As I was conversing with the hidden God, He gave me to see and understand that I should not be reflecting so much and building up fear of the difficulties which I might encounter. *[Jesus said:]* Know that I am with you; I bring about the difficulties, and I overcome them; in one instant, I can change a hostile disposition to one which is favorable to this cause. (788)

Seventh Insight

I want to live in the spirit of faith. I accept everything that comes my way as given me by the loving will of God, who sincerely desires my happiness. And so I will accept with submission and gratitude everything that God sends me. I will pay no attention to the voice of nature and to the promptings of self-love. Before each important action, I will stop to consider for a moment what relationship it has to eternal life and what may be the main reason for my undertaking it: is it for the glory of God, or for the good of my own soul, or for the good of the souls of others? (1549)

My Master, Lord Jesus, Hidden God, Sacred Heart, Living Host, My "Mother," My All, I want to grow closer to You by speaking, by listening, and by just being with You. Truly, Dear Jesus, of heaven on earth. Amen.

Seven Tips for Adoration

1. Come prepared. Bring whatever helps you pray well — your Bible, prayer book, spiritual reading, or rosary.

2. Slow your mind down and take a few deep breaths as you collect your thoughts. Begin your adoration by making yourself aware of the Lord's presence. Archbishop Fulton Sheen said that just resting in the Eucharistic presence works to make us more like Jesus.

3. Ask the Holy Spirit to guide your visit and be open to where He leads you. He's well known for nudging us in unexpected directions!

4. Take time to praise Jesus. Use the psalms or your favorite prayers or prayer book. Repeat a verse or line that strikes a chord with you. Then, too, you can just worship Him spontaneously. Tell Him what's on your mind and in your heart. Ask for forgiveness and intercede for others. Bring to the Lord those who have asked you to pray for them.

5. Let your posture express your praise. Engaging your body in prayer expresses your whole being. Kneeling, sitting, or standing are all appropriate.

6. In the silence, listen to the Lord. Ask Him what He's saying to you. Reflecting on Scripture — His Word — may be how He's telling you something.

7. Close your adoration with a spiritual communion and a prayer of thanksgiving for all Jesus has done for you. Thank Him for the time you've been able to spend with Him today.

Seven Obstacles to Adoration and How to Deal with Them

1. **Preoccupations.** Daily concerns may intrude on your adoration. Some adorers find it helpful to make a list of them and then leave it behind so that those thoughts don't tumble through their mind when they're trying to pray. (This doesn't refer to your "prayer list": the people and situations you *want* to be praying for.)

2. **Electronic devices.** Turn them off. Avoid even quiet digital interruptions or temptations. If need be, leave your cell phone at home or in

the car. (But this doesn't include using a device as a resource to read Scripture or favorite prayers.)

3. **Sin.** Just as we begin Mass with the *Confiteor* ("I confess to almighty God …"), it's a good idea to clear the decks for adoration by recognizing and acknowledging your sins, and asking for forgiveness. You can do that in your own words or with the traditional Act of Contrition or the *Confiteor*.

4. **Drowsiness.** You may find yourself falling asleep. Even though St. Thérèse of Lisieux said the Lord doesn't mind our napping at prayer, you may want to prevent it by standing. Picking a time for adoration when you're better rested may help. If you do "nod off" in prayer? That's okay.

5. **Not accustomed to silence.** Given the noise you endure all the time, you may have to get used to silence. Be patient with yourself as you become better at spending some quiet time just beholding the Lord in his Eucharistic presence. Listen, and let Him speak to you in your heart.

6. **Distractions.** When a stray, inconsequential thought slips into your mind, gently set it aside. However, sometimes the Lord "distracts" us with a concern He wants us to pray for. If that seems to be the case, pray for it as a way of returning to adoration.

7. **Dryness.** You may go through times when you don't sense the Lord's presence or don't feel like praying. You're not alone! Saints have written of it happening to them. Blessed Julian of Norwich advised saying prayers of thanksgiving to get the spiritual juices flowing again.

Contemporary Popes on Eucharistic Adoration

St. John Paul II

"May we always celebrate the Holy Eucharist with fervor. May we dwell long and often in adoration before Christ in the Eucharist. May we sit at the 'school' of the Eucharist."

— Letter to Priests, Holy Thursday, March 23, 2000

"Visit the Lord in that 'heart to heart' contact that is Eucharistic Adoration. Day after day, you will receive new energy to help you to bring comfort to the suffering and peace to the world."

— Message to Youth at World Youth Day,
Toronto, Canada, 2002

"If in our time Christians must be distinguished above all by the 'art of prayer,' how can we not feel a renewed need to spend time in spiritual converse, in silent adoration, in heartfelt love before Christ present in the Most Holy Sacrament? How often, dear brothers and sisters, have I experienced this, and drawn from it strength, consolation, and support!"

— *Ecclesia de Eucharistia*
("The Church from the Eucharist"), 2003

Pope Emeritus Benedict XVI

"Adoration means saying: 'Jesus, I am yours. I will follow you in my life, I never want to lose this friendship, this communion with you.'

I could also say that adoration is essentially an embrace with Jesus in which I say to him: 'I am yours, and I ask you, please stay with me always.' "

— Catechetical Meeting with Children Who Had Received
First Communion During the Year, October 15, 2005

"Receiving the Eucharist means adoring the One whom we receive. Precisely in this way and only in this way do we become one with him. Therefore, the development of Eucharistic adoration, as it took shape during the Middle Ages, was the most consistent consequence of the Eucharistic mystery itself: only in adoration can profound and true acceptance develop. And it is precisely this personal act of encounter with the Lord that develops the social mission which is contained in the Eucharist and desires to break down barriers, not only the barriers between the Lord and us but also and above all those that separate us from one another."

— Address to the Roman Curia, December 22, 2005

"There is another aspect of prayer which we need to remember: silent contemplation…. Have we perhaps lost something of the art of listening? Do you leave space to hear God's whisper, calling you forth into goodness? Friends, do not be afraid of silence or stillness, listen to God, adore him in the Eucharist. Let his word shape your journey as an unfolding of holiness."

— Meeting with Young People and Seminarians,
St. Joseph Seminary, Yonkers, New York, April 19, 2008

Pope Francis

"In the adoration of the Blessed Sacrament, Mary says to us: 'Look at my son Jesus, keep your gaze fixed on him, listen to him, speak with him. He is gazing at you with love. Do not be afraid! He will teach you to follow him and to bear witness to him in all that you do, whether great and small, in your family life, at work, at times of celebration. He will teach you to go out of yourself and to look upon others with love, as he did. He loved you and loves you, not with words but with deeds.' "

— On the Occasion of the Prayer Vigil
at the Shrine of Divine Love, October 12, 2013

"So let us ask ourselves this evening, in adoring Christ who is really present in the Eucharist: do I let myself be transformed by him? Do I let the Lord who gives himself to me, guide me to going out ever more from my little enclosure, in order to give, to share, to love him and others?"

— Homily at Mass on the Solemnity of Corpus Christi,
May 30, 2013

"What I really prefer is adoration in the evening, even when I get distracted and think of other things, or even fall asleep praying. In the evening then, between seven and eight o'clock, I stay in front of the Blessed Sacrament for an hour in adoration. But I pray mentally even when I am waiting at the dentist or at other times of the day."

— Interview with *La Civiltà Cattolica*,
September 19, 2013

Twenty-First-Century Adorers

"I Was So Nervous That I Would Do Adoration 'Wrong' "

"I've been going to adoration for more than ten years now. I remember when I first started, I was so nervous that I would do adoration 'wrong.' I thought I had to kneel the entire time that I was there and that if I didn't have a whole hour to give Jesus then I shouldn't even bother to go.

"I've since learned how wrong I was about all of that. I now kneel when I first get there, but then I can sit with the book I brought, my journal, or my rosary or chaplet (I have quite a collection of both). Sometimes I just sit quietly and chitchat with Jesus.

"Adoration is like going to the 'school of Jesus.' I've learned things about God and the Catholic Faith that nobody had ever taught me. Either through the materials I bring with me, through my reading of Scripture, or just through that time with Him, I feel like I get insights and information that I wouldn't have if I hadn't spent that time there.

"It's not that Jesus can't teach me elsewhere; there's just something about sitting in the presence of Christ. It's where heaven and earth collide, and God — in those moments — really shows His glory and His strength. As St. Teresa of Ávila said, 'There are times when, tired from our travels, we experience that the Lord calms our faculties and quiets the soul. As though by signs, He gives us a clear foretaste of what will be given to those He brings to His kingdom.'

"There's one more 'chapter' in my adoration story. While I began making visits alone, later my husband came to join me, and now we go together. I'm sure his time before Our Lord in the Blessed Sacrament helped him hear Jesus' calling him to the permanent diaconate!"

— Allison, an adorer for twelve years

"This Doing-God's-Will Stuff Is Challenging"

"After each of my visits with Jesus, I leave with a message or idea about how I can improve and really reach for holiness. During the week, I find Jesus giving me opportunities to practice what He taught me during the hour. One week I might try hard not to complain about things that go wrong. (Actually, I'm still working on that one.) Another week I might vow to say 'yes' to every request made of me … without hesitation. I notice that everyday duties take on a different and fuller meaning.

"Then, too, I have an increased readiness not only to agree to God's will but also to look for it. This doing-God's-will stuff is challenging at times, but very quickly He shows me that if I give in, it always turns out for the best."

— Carla, an adorer for twenty-nine years

"No Matter Where I Am in the Monastery, He's Nearby"

"My entire twenty-four years of religious life has been spent within one hundred feet of Jesus in the Most Blessed Sacrament. No matter where I am in the monastery, He's nearby, and especially close when I'm in the chapel, adoring His Eucharistic Presence. Not some kind of passive object in the Sacred Host for our adoration, He's alive. He's the very same Jesus that Our Lady and St. Joseph cherished, the one who died for us on the cross. I always have need of contact with Jesus, and my daily encounter with Him in the Eucharist fills me with gladness and is vital to my existence.

"Intimate friendship, unswerving spousal love, hopefulness, a foretaste of heaven, and a pledge of eternal life are just some of the blessings He generously shares with me in that chapel and in that monastery. Despite my unworthiness, when I'm with Jesus — as God and as man — I know that His glance rests upon me with infinite love.

"I'm never closer to Him than when I am in His Divine Presence of the Most Holy Eucharist and when I'm privileged to receive Him in Holy Communion."

— Mother Marie André, PCPA, an adorer for twenty-six years

"I Press Close to Jesus, Expecting to Become More Like Him."

"I like to spend time in silence before the Lord at adoration. St. Gregory of Nyssa said that just being in His presence allows God to restore the image in which He made me. So, I press close to Jesus, expecting to become more like Him, but I think it's going to take a long while. I also listen to hear if He wants to say something to me — and occasionally He gives me a word of encouragement or direction."

— Anthony, an adorer for eleven years

"Visiting Jesus Is Like Calling Your Mom ... to Share Your Day"

"I've been visiting Our Lord in the Blessed Sacrament for more than two decades. I try to go for an hour every day, but of course, there are some exceptions. Still, I'm *very* protective of that time.

"Visiting Jesus is like calling your mom or a family member to share your day or concerns. It's all about love! I can't be in front of Jesus without the healing rays of His love and mercy transforming my soul. If my goal is to be more like Him, this is a perfect way to allow Him to help.

"I may not notice Him 'working' on me, but I know He's given me so many tools to get me to heaven. Especially the Mass, the sacraments, and Eucharistic devotion. My 'little visits' are one tool, one way, He's guiding me to heaven."

— Natalie, an adorer for twenty-five years

A Father-Daughter Adoration "Team"

Daughter: "I Can Tell God Anything…. This Amazes Me!"

"When I go to adoration, I'm able to share my feelings, my thoughts, my sins, my problems, and my darkest secrets. I can tell God anything, and He'll listen. This *amazes* me! God is so patient. He'll forgive anyone, and forgive that person over and over again.

"When I go to adoration, I feel a sense of relief. I make mistakes daily, and adoration lifts that weight off my shoulders as I confess my sins to our ever-merciful God.

"Here's a tip I try to use during adoration: After you're done sharing your heart with God, give Him thanks and praise Him for what He's already done."

— Julia, an adorer for three years

Father: "It's Just the Two of Us. And Our Lord"

"Adoration time — and my coaching her basketball team — are our only father-daughter time outside the home. But, with adoration, it's just the two of us.

"And Our Lord.

"He asks me to be a living host, to love those who are the most difficult to love, to bear their wounds in Him and with Him. My vocation is my marriage and my family. Jesus wants me to be the image of our Heavenly Father to the family He entrusted to me, and I can only do this by learning and listening to Jesus; to His bride, the Church; and to the Holy Spirit. Mary and the saints can lead me.

"Julia and I find rest in Our Lord's love and mercy. During adoration, the two of us quietly listen and empty ourselves of ourselves so that — to quote 1 Kings 19:12 — we can better hear God's 'still small voice.' "

— Micah, an adorer for three years

Glossary of Adoration Terms

Benediction of the Blessed Sacrament: A devotional service to Christ in the Eucharist that includes the Blessed Sacrament being placed in a monstrance on an altar and incensed. It can also feature scriptural readings, silent prayer, and hymns (traditionally *O Salutaris Hostia* and *Tantum Ergo*). The priest blesses the people with the monstrance.

Corpus Christi **(Latin for "the Body of Christ"):** The solemnity of Corpus Christi commemorates the institution of the Eucharist and is traditionally celebrated on the Thursday after Trinity Sunday. In many dioceses, the celebration has been transferred to the Sunday following Trinity Sunday. It can include a Eucharistic procession.

Exposition of the Blessed Sacrament: The ceremony in which a priest or deacon removes the Sacred Host from the tabernacle and places it on the altar for adoration.

First Friday: A set of devotions to the Sacred Heart of Jesus, who granted to all who received Holy Communion on nine First Fridays of the month that they would receive the grace of final repentance, that they would not die in His displeasure, nor without receiving the sacraments. Some parishes celebrate First Fridays with Eucharistic Adoration and Benediction of the Most Blessed Sacrament, a beautiful way to deepen the devotion to the Sacred Heart.

Forty Hours Devotion: A forty-hour period of continuous prayer made before the Blessed Sacrament in solemn exposition in memory of the forty hours during which the body of Our Lord remained in the tomb. As practiced today, the devotion probably dates back to sixteenth-century Milan.

Holy Hour: A pious devotion consisting of mental and vocal prayer with exposition of the Blessed Sacrament. It draws its inspiration from Christ's words to the apostles in the Garden of Gethsemane: "So, could you not watch with me one hour?" (Mt 26:40).

Indulgence: "A remission before God of the temporal punishment due to sins whose guilt has already been forgiven, which the faithful Christian who is duly disposed gains under certain prescribed conditions through the action of the Church, which, as the minister of redemption, dispenses and applies with authority the treasury of the satisfactions of Christ and the saints" (CCC 1471). A partial indulgence is granted the Christian faithful when they visit the Blessed Sacrament for the purpose of adoration. When this is done for at least half an hour, the indulgence is a plenary one.

Luna: A circular container made of glass and gilded metal used to hold the Sacred Host securely in place in the center of the monstrance. (Also called a lunette.)

Monstrance: The receptacle in which the Sacred Host is exposed during Eucharistic Adoration, Benediction, or Eucharistic processions.

Nocturnal Adoration: A form of devotion in which participants offer adoration before the exposed Blessed Sacrament during the hours of the night.

Perpetual Adoration: A Eucharistic devotion in which members of a parish (or other group) unite to have at least one person present for adoration before the Blessed Sacrament (in most cases, with the Sacred Host exposed), twenty-four hours a day, seven days a week.

Procession: In general, a church procession is a traditional religious ritual in which the participants travel on foot from one place to another giving praise and thanks to God. A Eucharistic procession features the Blessed Sacrament being carried in a monstrance at the head of the formation, often under a canopy. For example, the celebration of the solemnity of Corpus Christi can include a Eucharistic procession.

Sanctuary Lamp: A candle kept burning in a church or chapel to indicate the presence of the Blessed Sacrament. The candle is typically placed in a red container.

Tabernacle: The receptacle in which the Blessed Sacrament is held in reserve in churches and chapels. It is immovable, solid, locked, and located in a prominent place.

Bibliography and Acknowledgments

Flynn, Vinny. *7 Secrets of the Eucharist.* Stockbridge, MA: MercySong, 2006.

Guernsey, Daniel P. *Adoration: Eucharistic Texts and Prayers Throughout Church History.* San Francisco: Ignatius, 1999.

Kieninger, Fr. Titus, O.R.C. *The Angels in the Diary of Saint Faustina Kowalska.* Carrollton, OH: Order of the Holy Cross, 2014.

Kolbe, St. Maximilian. *Stronger Than Hatred: A Collection of Spiritual Writings.* New York: New City Press, 1988.

Kosicki, George, W., C.S.B. *Mercy Minutes. Daily Gems of St. Faustina to Transform Your Prayer Life.* Stockbridge, MA: Marian Press, 2006.

———. *Revelations of Divine Mercy: Daily Readings from the Diary of Blessed Faustina Kowalska.* Copyright © 1996 by The Congregation of Marians of the Immaculate Conception of the Blessed Virgin Mary. Ann Arbor, MI: Servant Publications, 1996.

———. *Thematic Concordance to the Diary of St. Maria Faustina Kowalska.* Stockbridge, MA: Marian Press, 2015.

———, with David Came. *Faustina, Saint for Our Times: A Personal Look at Her Life, Spirituality, and Legacy.* Stockbridge, MA: Marian Press, 2011.

Kowalska, St. Maria Faustina. *Diary of Saint Maria Faustina Kowalska.* Stockbridge, MA: Marian Press, 1987.

Manelli, Fr. Stefano, O.F.M. Conv., S.T.D. *Jesus, Our Eucharistic Love.* Neapoli: 1973.

McNeil, Brian, C.R.V. *The Master is Here: Biblical Reflections on Eucharistic Adoration.* Dublin: Veritas Publications, 1997.

Siepak, Sister M. Elżbieta, O.L.M., and Sister M. Nazaria Dlubak, O.L.M. *The Spirituality of St. Faustina.* Kraków, Poland: Misericordia Publications, 2000.

Tarnawska, Maria. *Sister Faustina Kowalska: Her Life and Mission.* Stockbridge, MA: Marian Press, 2000.

Tesnière, Rev. A. *The Eucharistic Christ: Reflections and Considerations on the Blessed Sacrament.* New York: Benzinger Brothers, 1897.

Resources

For information about the National Shrine of The Divine Mercy and to become a Friend of Mercy, go to www.thedivinemercy.org.

Association of Marian Helpers
Eden Hill
Stockbridge, MA 01263

Holy Souls Sodality
c/o Association of Marian Helpers
Eden Hill
Stockbridge, MA 01263
www.prayforsouls.org

For memberships, and to obtain Masses and Gregorian Masses:

Pious Union of St. Joseph
953 East Michigan Avenue
Grass Lake, MI 49240
(517) 522-8017
www.pusj.org

About the Cover

Graphic designer Garrett Fosco does an amazing interpretation of a vision St. Faustina saw on June 20, 1935. She wrote:

Once, the [Divine Mercy] image was being exhibited over the altar during the Corpus Christi procession.... When the priest exposed the Blessed Sacrament, and the choir began to sing, the rays from the image pierced the Sacred Host and spread out all over the world. Then I heard these words: These rays of mercy will pass through you, just as they have passed through this Host, and they will go out through all the world. At these words, profound joy invaded my soul. (441)

When I was in church waiting for confession, I saw the same rays issuing from the monstrance and spreading throughout the church.... [The rays shone out] to both sides and returned again to the monstrance. Their appearance was bright and transparent like crystal. I asked Jesus that He deign to light the fire of His love in all souls that were cold. Beneath these rays a heart will grow warm even if it were like a block of ice; even if it were hard as a rock, it will crumble into dust. (370)

In a similar way, may Christ's rays of mercy pass through you during your times of adoration — whether before the Eucharist or in private — and go out through all the world. And may profound joy invade your soul and the souls of all.

— SUSAN

About the Author

SUSAN TASSONE has long been a passionate champion for the holy souls in purgatory and is recognized as leading a worldwide "purgatory movement."

The award-winning author of ten best-sellers, including *St. Faustina Prayer Book for the Holy Souls in Purgatory*, Susan makes speaking appearances throughout the country. She's a frequent and popular guest on national radio and television programs as well as social media. In 2013, she was featured in the groundbreaking documentary *Purgatory: The Forgotten Church* and was on the cover of *Catholic Digest* magazine in 2017.

She also continues to work tirelessly to raise donations for Masses for the holy souls.

Susan holds a master's degree in religious education from Loyola University Chicago and had the honor and privilege of being granted two private audiences with St. John Paul II, who bestowed a special blessing on her and her ministry for the holy souls.

Learn more at: susantassone.com.

Other Books by Susan Tassone

- **The Rosary for the Holy Souls in Purgatory:** This little book slips easily into your pocket, so it can go with you anywhere. Make praying for the holy souls a regular part of your devotional life. **ID# T25**

- **Thirty-Day Devotions for the Holy Souls:** This book offers comfort to those who are grieving and gives them a personal and powerful method of praying for their departed family member or friend. **ID# T103**

- **The Way of the Cross for the Holy Souls in Purgatory:** This one-of-a-kind combination of the traditional prayers of the Stations of the Cross and scriptural reflections focuses on Christ's passion and death. **ID# T192**

- **Praying with the Saints for the Holy Souls in Purgatory:** This inspiring book shows how you can join the saints in this act of divine charity, thereby attaining spiritual gifts for acts done for the souls that cry out to us for relief. **ID# T833**

- **Prayers, Promises, and Devotions for the Holy Souls in Purgatory:** Become a prayer warrior on behalf of the suffering souls in purgatory, and bring comfort to them and to yourself along the way. **ID# T1254**

- **Day by Day for the Holy Souls in Purgatory: 365 Reflections:** Every day we have another opportunity to pray for the holy souls in purgatory, and Susan gives you a unique tool to do just that. **ID# T1577**

- **St. Faustina Prayer Book for the Holy Souls in Purgatory:** Susan turns to a passionate and powerful guide to help us pray for the holy souls in purgatory, St. Faustina Kowalska. Includes devotions, prayers, novenas, and the wisdom of St. Faustina. **ID# T1759**

- **St. Faustina Prayer Book for the Conversion of Sinners**: Susan invites you to learn how to live the message of conversion daily, to avoid purgatory, and to become more faithful in praying for others. **ID# T1815**